The European Union and the Middle East

Søren Dosenrode
and Anders Stubkjær

★ UACES ★

SHEFFIELD ACADEMIC PRESS
A Continuum imprint
LONDON • NEW YORK

1006409392

Copyright © 2002 Sheffield Academic Press
A Continuum imprint

Published by Sheffield Academic Press Ltd
The Tower Building, 11 York Road, London SE1 7NX
370 Lexington Avenue, New York NY 10017-6550

www.SheffieldAcademicPress.com
www.continuumbooks.com

British Library Cataloguing-in-Publication Data

A catalogue record for this book is available from the British Library

Typeset by Sheffield Academic Press
Printed on acid-free paper in Great Britain by MPG Books Ltd, Bodmin, Cornwall

ISBN 0-8264-6089-5 (paperback)
     0-8264-6088-7 (hardback)

Contents

Boxes

Figures

Tables

Series Foreword

The European Union aspires to play an increasingly influential role as a global actor and this is particularly true in relation to its near neighbours in the Middle East. What is often not appreciated is the long history of EC/EU involvement in the area and the evolution of its policy in response to changes in the international environment. This book is therefore a very welcome addition to the Contemporary European Studies series and will help to provide the necessary context for an understanding of the complex policy issues that the EU is currently facing in the region. It also complements the very popular earlier book by Fraser Cameron on the EU's Common Foreign and Security Policy. Further books planned for the series include studies of the EU's relations with both Asia and Russia.

The Contemporary European Studies series was launched in 1998 by the University Association of Contemporary European Studies (UACES), the foremost UK organization bringing together academics and practitioners interested in the study of contemporary Europe. The objective of the series is to provide authoritative texts dealing with a wide range of important issues of interest to both those studying and teaching about European integration and professionals wishing to keep up with current developments. Observant readers may well have noticed a change in the imprint on the spine of the books reflecting the acquisition of Sheffield Academic Press by Continuum in September 2001. Future books will be published under a joint Continuum/UACES imprint with both parties working closely together to develop both the reputation and international sales of the series.

I am very grateful to Clive Archer for encouraging the authors to embark on the writing of the book and providing editorial comment at every stage of its gestation.

Jackie Gower
Series Editor

Preface

A study of the European Union's relations with the Middle East is interesting because it will be a reflection of what has been faced by the EU in gradually establishing its position in external relations and its foreign policy mechanism. In other words, it mirrors the EU's slowly emerging role as an international actor.

The Middle East[1] was on the agenda of the first meeting of the European Political Cooperation, and, with only a few exceptions, it has remained there ever since. The EU's behaviour vis-à-vis the conflicts in the Middle East reflects to a large degree the conditions under which the EU developed its actorness. From an international perspective, the relationship demonstrates how the international system in general and other international actors in particular have influenced the actions of the EU. From an EU internal perspective, a study of the relationship between the EU and the Middle East will exhibit the schisms between coalitions of states within the EU. In the light of this, the book is an analysis of the EU as an international actor, as well as an analysis of the EU's relations to the Middle East.

Our thesis is that the EU's foreign policy contains some inherent contradictions. The EU strives to project itself on the international scene, and it seeks continuously to enhance its presence and influence in international politics, among other things, through the continued development and refinement of its arsenal of foreign policy tools. Even though the EU possesses the necessary mechanisms for policy-making, as well as instruments to implement the policies, the EU's efforts to formulate coherent and independent foreign policies are often undermined by two things. First, in relation to the Middle East, the EU lacks

1.   In line with Hourani, we define the Middle East as: Bahrain, Egypt, Iraq, Jordan, Kuwait, Lebanon, Oman, the Palestinian Occupied Territories, Qatar, Saudi Arabia, Syria, United Arab Emirates, Yemen and the State of Israel (Hourani 1994: 508-509).

the political will and interests to keep the relations to the region high on the political agenda, and due to domestic interests it is an extremely difficult exercise to reach a consensus. Secondly, the EU is suffering from the unchallenged hegemony of the USA in the region—and elsewhere—which limits the EU's ability to manoeuvre.

The book is in three parts: the first two chapters consist of introductions to the EU as an international actor (Chapter 1), and to the Arab Middle East (Chapter 2). The second part of the book is an analysis of the developments in European–Middle Eastern relations between 1950 and 1991. Chapter 3 focuses on relations between 1950 and 1969, Chapter 4 on EC/EU–Middle East relations between 1969 and 1991. Chapter 5 then deals with EU–Middle East relations between 1991 and 2000. In the third part of the book, we present a series of reflections on some of the most central issues and challenges facing the EU and the Middle East today.

The basis of this book is research conducted during 1998–2002.[2] Apart from the extensive literature on this topic, we have collected material for this book through archive research and by conducting interviews in, *inter alia*, Brussels where we met a number of centrally placed persons from the EU institutions, the most important European embassies, and the embassies of the Middle Eastern region. These talks have proven very useful to our work, and we gladly acknowledge our gratitude to the persons who shared their valuable insights with us.

In addition, a Web address is given in some of the notes and references in the book. This means that the article has been collected from the Internet and the page number may in some cases differ from the original publication.

We have aimed to use the EC/EU abbreviations according to the period we cover, but the EU abbreviation is used more frequently and does not always correspond with the historically correct EC title. This is mainly to facilitate reading.

2.   We would like to thank the University of Aalborg, Institute for History, Social and International Studies, as well as the Danish Institute of International Affairs for their financial support. At the same time we would like to thank Ms Helle Weiergang BA, Ms Julie Larsen MA, and Mr Bill Davey MA, for their help with the manuscript.

Abbreviations

CAP	Common Agricultural Policy
CCP	Common Commercial Policy
CET	Common External Tariff
CFSP	Common Foreign and Security Policy
CEC	Commission of the European Communities
COREPER	Committee of Permanent Representatives
COREU	Correspondant Européen (EPC Communications Network)
CSCM	Conference of Security and Cooperation for the Mediterranean
CUP	Committee of Union and Progress
DG	Directorate-General
DoP	Declaration of Principles
EEC	European Economic Community
EC	European Community
ECHO	European Communities Humanitarian Office
ECJ	European Court of Justice
ECSC	European Coal and Steel Community
EDC	European Defence Community
EFTA	European Free Trade Association
EP	European Parliament
EPC	European Political Cooperation
EU	European Union
GAC	General Affairs Council
GATT	General Agreement on Tariffs and Trade
GCC	Gulf Cooperation Council
GDP	gross domestic product
GMP	Global Mediterranean Policy
GNP	gross national product
IDF	Israel Defense Forces
IEA	International Energy Agency
IGC	Intergovernmental Conference
INF	Intermediate-range Nuclear Forces
MEP	Member of the European Parliament
NATO	North Atlantic Treaty Organization
NGO	non-governmental organization
OECD	Organization for Economic Cooperation and Development

OPEC	Organization of Petroleum Exporting Countries
OSCE	Organization for Security and Cooperation in Europe
PLO	Palestine Liberation Organization
PNA	Palestinian National Authority
PPEWU	Policy Planning and Early Warning Unit
QMV	qualified majority voting
REDWG	Regional Economic Development Working Group
SALT	Strategic Arms Limitation Talks
SCR	Common Service for External Relations
SEA	Single European Act
TEC	Treaty Establishing the European Community
TEU	Treaty on European Union
UAE	United Arab Emirates
UAR	United Arab Republic
UN	United Nations
UNSCR	United Nations Security Council Resolution
WEU	Western European Union
WTO	World Trade Organization

1 |

The European Union's Foreign Policy: The Development of an International Actor

External Relations: Interests and Policies

It may sound banal to start out by stating that the development of the EU's foreign policy has been parallel to that of the EU itself. But it is important to remember that the EU has developed from the European Coal and Steel Community (1950) into a Union which, at the beginning of the new millennium, possesses many of the attributes normally associated with a state. This development from international organization to state-like entity has taken over 40 years, and it is still under construction. Thus the Union's foreign policy is bound to be embryonic and often incoherent in many fields. In retrospect, the last 40 years of European integration reveals a surprisingly straight line, from the visions of the 'founding fathers' until today's EU. This chapter thus starts out by looking at the historic development of the Union's foreign policy, looking at the motives behind the creation of a foreign policy, before tracing the development of the Union's actorness, and ending up by analysing the EU's foreign policy today.

Currently, the foreign policy capability of the Union consists of two parts: a supranational part mainly the responsibility of the Commission, and an 'intergovernmental' part, mainly the responsibility of the Council of Ministers. The word 'mainly' indicates that there are many grey zones and overlaps, as we shall see later. These grey zones disappear when all of the foreign political actors meet as the European Council, where all the Heads of State and Government and the President of the European Commission are present. As the European Council *de facto* constitutes something looking very much like a government and as the Maastricht and Amsterdam Treaties successively have strengthened the actor capability of the Union, it is now right to use the term European Foreign and Security Policy (EFSP), not only the term 'external relations' (Dosenrode 2000: 69).[1]

The Creation of a Foreign Policy Mechanism

The years immediately after the end of the Second World War did not meet the expectations of those who had trusted in the United Nations as guarantor for a new peaceful world. Again economic and political insecurity prevailed. What had been a not-very-secret rivalry between the Soviet Union and the Western Allies during the war, revealed itself as outright hostility, close to war. For more than 300 years, Europe had been able to project power outside its own borders in such a way that it was possible to talk about Europe ruling the world. This situation ended after the Second World War. Europe was ruled by two superpowers, one Eurasian power and one American, as had been predicted by French Prime Minister Aristide Briand in the 1920s.

To prevent a new French-German war, the means for war—coal and steel for arms and armour—were to be put under the supranational control of the ECSC. Thus today's EU was founded upon a political vision of peace and prosperity with a direct connection to Aristide Briand's aborted inter-war years' proposal and the other peace plans of the preceding centuries.

One year later, the French Minister of Defence Robert Pleven, inspired by Jean Monnet, suggested a European Defence Community (EDC), based on common institutions comprising: a European minister of defence, responsible to a council of ministers, an assembly, and a common budget, but this idea failed (Dinan 1999: 26). The ECSC, created by the Treaty of Paris in 1951, and the European Economic Community and the European Atomic Energy Commission, both created by the two Treaties of Rome in 1957, had supranational elements in them. These were challenged by President de Gaulle during the 1960s. De Gaulle's motives were to create a union of states. This 'Europe of the Fatherlands' would in the long run be strong enough to challenge the existing bipolar situation, that is, the joint hegemony of

---

1.   The Nice Treaty did not strengthen the CFSP directly but it did it indirectly as it strengthened the Union's statehood. This development has proceeded after the terrorist actions on 11 September 2001. A senior diplomat told one of the authors that 11 September has resulted in an integration leap equivalent to five years within the fields of CFSP, Justice and Home Affairs.

the Soviet Union and, especially, the USA over Europe. De Gaulle had secured the support of Konrad Adenauer before informing the other four governments of the idea, which all supported it, apart from the Netherlands. The French ambassador in Copenhagen, Charles Fouchet, was assigned chairman of the committee set up to draft a treaty (Dosenrode 1993: 187-88).

De Gaulle's plan was to create a kind of confederation, toning down the supranational parts of the already existing community. The confederation was to include cooperation on the already established fields, but also education, culture, science, and most importantly, foreign affairs and defence policy. The focal point should be regular meetings of the Heads of State and Government, a council of ministers, served by one or more commissions of senior civil servants, and advised by an assembly. Military integration should thus take place within the framework of the confederation, not in NATO. This French proposal was not implemented as it was opposed by the Dutch and Belgians. What came out of this exercise was the Elysée Treaty of 1963, in which France and Germany promised to consult each other on all questions of foreign affairs, before making decisions. Although not what de Gaulle had wanted, this treaty has been important for the further development of the foreign political dimension of the strong partnerships in the EU, the 'Bonn-Paris Axis' (Dosenrode 1993: 203-206).

The Birth of the European Political Cooperation: Hague 1969
The 'very cold phase' of the Cold War had changed into the decade of détente (1969–79), where the two superpowers tried to manage their relations through agreements and negotiations. This loosening up of the tight bipolarity incited the Europeans to try to work on foreign political coordination, with the aim of being heard in world politics. This seemed meaningful from a European point of view, as a number of incidents had shown that the Six[2] were not able to agree on a common stand, and that European affairs were still decided outside Europe. One incident illustrating the disagreement among the Six, was the Six Days War in June 1967 (discussed in more detail in Chapter 3). The Six could not agree on a common stand towards the conflict, and there were also divergences between France and a potential EC member, the UK, too. Added to this, the Soviet invasion of Czechoslovakia in 1968 had

2. Belgium, the Federal Republic of Germany, France, Italy, Luxembourg and the Netherlands.

clearly shown that the destiny of European states was not decided by Europeans, but by the two superpowers outside Europe. But de Gaulle's attitude towards the UK and European integration in general blocked development. Thus nothing happened until de Gaulle resigned in 1969, opening the possibility for an extension of the European Community of the Six to a Community of Ten (to include Denmark, Ireland, Norway and the UK). As the Norwegian population decided not to join the EC, the Six became the Nine. At the summit in the Hague in December 1969 the Heads of State and Government asked the foreign ministers of the Six to report on the best way of promoting political unity, within the context of the enlargement.

The EC had by then become the world's largest trading bloc, economic integration seemed successful and was still in progress. By 1968, the transition period which limited the Commission's external responsibilities had ended, and the Commission could assume an active role in external relations. The Commission had especially two policies at its disposal: the Common Commercial Policy and the Common External Tariff. In spite of this, the Common Commercial Policy had only progressed very slowly. Since 1962, the Commission had occasionally made proposals to the Council of Ministers for harmonization of the national commercial policies, but the member states were more than reluctant to give up what they perceived as freedom of action in favour of some artificial 'European interest'. But the outside world began thinking of the EC as an international actor due to its mere presence, and was expecting this emergent trade-superpower to behave as such. They were supported in their expectations by seeing the Commission representing the member states during the Dillon Round (1960–62) and the Kennedy Round (1964–67) under the General Agreement on Tariffs and Trade (GATT). Thus, successful internal integration created an external expectation for some kind of orchestrated foreign policy of the EC.

Another important motivation for progress in the external sphere was the political aspect. Jean Monnet had expected foreign policy integration to come at a late stage, but had felt forced by the development in Korea to introduce the idea of a Common Defence Community including a European Political Community. Since then there had been occasional voices pleading for foreign policy cooperation to strengthen the integration process as a whole. These ideas constitute another important motive for the Hague Conference.

At the Hague in 1969, the Heads of State and Government had expressed the view that Europe was to prepare to take its place in the world in accordance with its tradition and mission. The member states all expressed a wish to strengthen and complete the integration of the EC, and the summit as such belongs to the milestones in the history of today's EU. It was in this spirit the foreign ministers started out with three basic statements (Birkelbach 1972: 37-38). They stated:

> it is necessary to give the will for political unification a concrete form, the development in the economic integration process necessitates a similar development within the political, aiming at giving Europe the ability to speak with one voice, and Europe has to prepare itself for exercising responsibility over the growing importance the world demands of it.

Political cooperation along these lines would, according to the Hague report, expand integration, as well as create an understanding for its necessity among the peoples of Europe (Davignon or Luxembourg report). In short, the foreign ministers made the following suggestions: (1) the governments should consult each other on all important foreign political issues; (2) the member states should have the right to suggest political consultations on all questions of their choice; (3) the foreign ministers should meet at least twice a year, with meetings prepared by a political committee. Further, they suggested that this committee should have the directors of the political departments of the foreign offices as members, and should meet at least four times a year to prepare the meetings of the foreign ministers and to execute their decisions. The report did not include obligations to take any decisions or to act in accordance with the common points of view. Equally important, there was no role for the EEC Commission to play. The report merely stated that, in the cases where the work of the ministers affects the activities of the EC, the Commission would be requested to make its opinion clear (second part, V).

The report, which was drafted by Viscount Davignon, was accepted by the foreign ministers in October 1970, and the foreign ministers met for their first meeting of the European Political Cooperation in November 1970 in Munich. It is worthwhile noting that one of the two topics on the agenda of the first EPC meeting was the Middle East; a topic which was to remain on the agenda.

The First Years of the European Political Cooperation
As indicated earlier, the first years of the EPC coincided with détente, the relaxation of the former tense relationship between the US and the USSR, as well as with the enlargement of the EEC. Détente partly built on the 'Ostpolitik' of German Chancellor Willy Brandt, and showed that European states could play an important, but only minor role in world politics. Détente was thus considered by some Europeans as an opportunity to profile the 'European way' of cooperation instead of confrontation.

But détente did not mean that peace prevailed all over the world. Tensions cooled off within Europe, but outside the US–Soviet rivalry continued. Especially in the Middle East the Israeli–Arab war in 1973 came close to bringing about a major confrontation involving both superpowers directly. The 1973 war showed that the US and Soviet had influence in the Middle East, but that they certainly did not rule undisputed. The aftermath of the 1973 war also had serious implications on the EEC and the EPC, as will be seen later (oil crisis). The détente period faded away as Soviet support for various Marxist-Leninist oriented regimes in the third world escalated (e.g., Ethiopia 1975, Angola 1978, Afghanistan 1978). In 1979, NATO decided to deploy Pershing II Cruise missiles in Europe if negotiations with the Soviet Union did not result in reducing what the West perceived as an unacceptable power imbalance, caused by Soviet deployment of SS-20 missiles. These tensions were further strained with the election of Ronald Reagan as US President in 1980. Thus the international environment of the EPC was tense from 1973 and onwards.

The first year the EC consisted of nine members was 1973; the year of both the first oil crisis and, seen from Europe, the rather tactless US initiative of 'the Year of Europe'. Both created enough dynamism for the summit in Copenhagen at the end of the year to make progress in the EPC process. The Copenhagen summit in December 1973 adopted both a report on the EPC and a declaration on European identity. The Copenhagen Report laid down the basic institutional and practical frame of the EPC, which lasted until the Maastricht Treaty was adopted 20 years later. According to the report, the purpose of the EPC was to secure consultations, exchange of information, improve mutual understanding and strengthen the loyalty among the Nine and when possible, take joint actions (*Bulletin of the EC* 9 [1973]: 14). The same report stressed that the Nine wanted to make a contribution to the equilibrium of power in the world, and that the EPC and the EC both should be seen in the context of the development of the European Communities.

Institutionally, the Copenhagen Report stipulated that the foreign ministers should increase the number of meetings from two to four per year, that the frequency of the meetings of the Political Committee should be increased, that each member state should have a European correspondent in the foreign office to take care of day-to-day work and prepare the meetings of the Political Committee. To accomplish these goals working parties were introduced, and the inter-foreign office communication network, the COREU, was established. In relation to the Commission the ministers simply stated that they appreciated the way the consultations agreed in the Luxembourg report had worked.

The declaration on European identity stressed the linkage between the EC and EPC, and the importance of the EPC as a tool for making a united Europe. The declaration clearly stressed the need for political cooperation: 'International developments and the growing concentration of power and responsibility in the hands of a very small number of great powers, mean that Europe must unite and speak increasingly with one voice, if it wants to make itself heard and play its proper role in the world' (*Bulletin of the EC* 12 [1973]: 122).

The reaction of the USA was as sharp as it could be, without upsetting the NATO alliance. Secretary of State Henry Kissinger expressed the US unease very clearly, and the result was an agreement on informal consultations. But the incident showed that the USA considered the potential of a European foreign policy as a genuine threat to its supremacy; the USA had an ambivalent attitude towards European integration; but foremost that the USA had a decisive say, in so far as the Nine complied with US wishes.

1973 also brought the beginning of the revision of the Yaoundé agreement. The Yaoundé initiative was tailored to suit former French and Belgian colonies mainly in Africa. With the inclusion of the UK in the EC, other former colonies with other needs were included too. As was agreed under the EC Treaty, it was the Commission which had the right of initiative, and thus submitted the first proposal to the Council of Ministers. It took until the beginning of 1975 to negotiate what was to be known as Lomé 1, running for five years until 1980 (Archer 1994: 152-53). In the meantime supranational external relations developed quietly. A number of trade agreements were concluded with the EFTA states, entering into force by January 1973, and the Commission represented the EC during the Tokyo Round of GATT.

The summits of the Heads of State and Government came to play a very important role in development of the EU. But it was not until the Paris summit of December 1974, that it was decided to create a European Council where Heads of State and Government would meet regularly. At the summit in Paris in December 1974 the Belgian Prime Minister, Leo Tindemans, was asked to write a report on the concept of 'the European Union'. It was delivered one year later. Europe was in a crisis and Tindemans' question was what the public expected from the EC. The first and most important answer to Tindemans' question was to have a voice towards the rest of the world (Tindemans 1976: 10-11):

> During my visits, it has appeared to me, that I meet a feeling of us being vulnerable and powerless... Our populations expect that the European Union speaks with one voice, when it is necessary and one expects it... Europe must...avoid the submission, the strong dependence which prevents it from expressing its own points of view. It has to rediscover a certain power over its own destiny...the need for Europe to speak with one voice in its relations with the United States is one of the main underlying reasons for the construction of Europe.

Tindemans suggested stronger coordination, and voting on measures in case unanimity could not be reached. Especially the latter did not go down very well with the Heads of State and Government in the Hague in November 1976, and consequently the report was shelved.

The oil crisis and the following economic crisis did provide the impulse which could close the ranks of the member states concerning EPC. On the contrary, the energy crisis caused the member states to fall back to old patterns of individual foreign policy actions as a response to clever OPEC policy (OPEC set up an embargo list of countries not receiving any oil). The following world economic crisis and the end of détente did not promote unity as some theories of integration such as federalism in its more vulgar form would suggest it should. Still, a 'sentiment' built up at the end of the 1970s that there was a need 'to do something', as Europe seemed utterly lost without any influence over her own destiny. Instead Europe was a pawn in the political chess game played by the USSR and USA (Nuttall 2000: 21).

At the beginning of the 1980s the 'Second Cold War' replaced détente and again there was a genuine fear of a nuclear war, fought out in 'the European theatre'. This fear was founded on three events: the US launch of the strategic defence initiative 'Star Wars'; martial law in Poland

1981; and the Soviet misinterpretation of the NATO exercise 'Able Archer' in 1983. All three events hinted at the possibility of nuclear destruction, if something should go wrong. The nightmare scenario was a nuclear destruction in Europe triggered off by non-European powers.

The first serious European attempt to strengthen Western Europe's voice in European affairs came from Germany and Italy. During 1981 German Foreign Minister Genscher and Italian Foreign Minister Colombo, separately, and later jointly, worked on a draft for a 'European Act'. The Genscher–Colombo plan envisaged a codification of the EPC, placing it under the European Council, alongside the EC. It also introduced security politics as an explicit topic for the EPC, including the possibility of an EC council of defence ministers (Nuttall 2000: 21). Denmark opposed both, as it looked like a strengthening of integration as well as the introduction of the security dimension; the latter posed a problem to the Irish government, too. And, as the general welcome was friendly but not excited in London in November 1981, the proposal was passed on to the foreign ministers for further consultations and clarifications.

The London Summit approved the London Report on the EPC, which had been on its way since November 1980. The report's tone is pragmatic and intergovernmental. The important elements are: institutional reinforcement, 'crisis management', security and political commitment, to which we will now turn (Nuttall 2000: 21). One problem of the intergovernmental approach of the EPC was the overburdening of the presidency, especially for the smaller member states. To create continuity and to help sharing the burden, the 'troika model' was introduced. The troika consisted of the President-in-Office, assisted by the previous presidency and following one. Assisted by the previous presidency and the one to follow, the President-in-Office could discuss answers to issues raised or they could undertake missions together. The idea was simple and worked well. The Commission should, as an innovation, be 'fully associated at all levels', to secure coordination with the external relations conducted within the EC framework. Another problem had been the lack of ability to react swiftly to foreign political developments. Thus, it was decided that, at the request of three member states, a meeting at foreign minister or at political director level could be called within 48 hours. The question of security was treated in a pragmatic way; it was agreed to create the possibility to meet and discuss the 'political aspects of security'. Vague formulation turned out to be the door-opener, letting in military security and defence policy in the subsequent treaties. The question of political commitment was stressed, when the Heads of State and Government stated their: 'commitment to consult partners before adopting final positions or launching national initiatives on all important questions of foreign policy' (London Report 1981: 2). This commitment describes a significant development compared with the Luxembourg and the Copenhagen reports.

The already mentioned initiative of foreign ministers Genscher and Colombo continued to be in the decision-making system, but it seemed as if neither Germany nor Italy really pushed it forward. It ended after several consultations, hearings and compromises at the June 1983 summit in Stuttgart, as a very vague and watered-down version: 'The Solemn Declaration on European Union'. Basically, it was a description of the *status quo*; no wonder it passed unnoticed. Referring to the situation in the international system, Ifestos (1987: 308-309) suggests two possible explanations of the meagre contents of the Solemn Declaration. The bipolar system was less stable and certain than it had been. This uncertainty left the European states with two possible strategies: further integration or concentration on other international groups or organizations (i.e. NATO). Ifestos concludes his analysis:

> The member states, faced with the enormity and complexity of the difficulties of such an undertaking [further integration] and the dangers involved if it is not carried through successfully, seem to have excluded defence and military matters from the European Community, which remains a 'civilian political actor'. Instead, the Member states opted for a mixed system...consisting of a controllable economic integration process, a selective and flexible concertation framework as regards foreign politics, and, within EPC, a cautious low profile examination of 'political' and 'economic' aspects of European security (1987: 309).

A *tour d'horizon* of the intentions of the large member states concerning the EPC and its future at the beginning of the 1980s produces the following result. According to de la Serre and Defarges (1983: 61) 'the French Government seems to have pursued two goals: on the one hand, to promote, within the European framework, a system close to French constitutional doctrine, and guided by the Heads of State and Government; and on the other, to preserve the unity and continuity of French foreign policy'. Quite the same attitude is found in Rummel and Wessels' analysis of Germany:

the Federal Republic used it [the EPC] to enhance its international position and to enlarge its freedom of manoeuvre...governments in Bonn would not have a major interest in strengthening Political Co-operation to an extent which would inhibit their newly gained 'freedom' (1983: 47).

Hill strikes the same chord in his analysis of Britain:

it is doubtful whether any party holding sway in Westminster would be willing to go much further in relinquishing national freedom of manoeuvre in international relations. As it stands, EPC is too good for British foreign policy for Britain to seek a genuinely European substitute (Hill 1983: 31).

Italy is the only one of the, then, four EC great powers to promote a supranational EPC stand. Bonvicini argues out of fear of too much national thinking and tendencies towards a directorate consisting of Germany, France and perhaps the UK, Italy would have preferred a supranational foreign policy (1983: 77-79). The development of the EPC seemed to suit the three most important members of the EC well. It served their diplomatic needs in three ways; it pooled their resources, it reflected a tendency towards multilateralism, and finally but most significantly it did not cost them anything in terms of freedom of action and sovereignty.

The Beginning of a New Era: The Single European Act
In 1984 the Commission launched the idea of creating a European Economic Area between the EFTA States and the EC, and in June in Fontainebleau, the question of the UK's budgetary contributions was solved. It was decided to create two *ad hoc* committees. One committee would make proposals for bringing the Community closer to its citizens, the other committee would find proposals for strengthening the cooperation in all fields. What made the change? There were several contributory factors. First, Europe was lagging behind Japan and the USA in questions of trade, competition and technology (Delor's Internal Market report). Secondly, there was an ideological shift in Europe in the direction of economic liberalism. Thirdly, the new Cold War created a feeling of helplessness among the European states. Fourthly, tensions arose between the USA and its European allies (the missile case, the pipeline case, the Euro–Arab dialogue and so on). Lastly, the Spinelli Report, the Draft Treaty Establishing the European Union, was passed by the European Parliament in February 1984. All together these factors constituted incentives for further integration, which made the member states feel obliged to act (e.g. Ifestos 1987: 328-47).

At the Milan summit (June 1985), the European Council debated the Commission's White Paper on the Internal Market (1992), and the Dooge report. The latter had, *inter alia*, suggested an intergovernmental conference (IGC), against the wishes of the UK, Danish and Greek members. Expectations were high. The Italian Presidency envisaged an IGC to create a new treaty or, as a minimum, tighten up and reform the old one. As agreement on an IGC could not be reached with consensus, the sensation came when Italy called for a vote. Never before had a decision in the European Council been decided by vote. Denmark, Greece and the UK voted against an IGC, the rest were in favour and an IGC was summoned.

The result of the IGC was the Single European Act (SEA) (*Single* because it was one document on both EC and EPC matters). Among the important results of the IGC were: (1) the codification of the EPC; (2) the introduction of qualified majority voting in a number of cases where unanimity had been the norm before (to make the preparation of the internal market programme work); (3) that the Luxembourg agreement of 1966 was not abolished; (4) the European Parliament (EP) was more closely involved in the decision-making process thus enhancing its power; and (5) the new modus for cooperation between the EP and the Council of Ministers. The text of the SEA concerning the EPC synthesized and summarized the various reports, declarations and daily working of the EPC into one legal text (Dosenrode 1993: 211-12).

This text itself did not mark a quantum jump to a higher level of integration, but did add the possibility of discussing the economic and political aspects of security, and it solved the problem of institutionalization by deciding to create a small EPC secretariat in Brussels. Thus, the small steps of the SEA created a new platform for the EPC's further development. In this context, the Commission for the first time was fully included in the EPC work (Article 30(3)(b)). Furthermore, the President-in-Office and the Commission were requested to secure coherence in the policies of the EPC and the EC. Thus ended the days where the Commission's civil servants had to find out when, where, and on what topic the EPC was meeting. Leo Tindemans commented on the EPC in a speech in Rome, 4 March 1987: 'albeit the act was the product of simple negotiations, it unquestionably had to be regarded as worthwhile. But as a basic treaty for the next thirty years of European unification, it was disappointing.' Tindemans was right; and wrong. One always has to keep in mind that it is seldom the *treaties* which create the dynamics in the foreign relations field of the EU. Treaties merely codify what is already praxis. The SEA did, however, cement the dynamism in the integration process and it laid the foundations for the Maastricht and Amsterdam Treaties, first by introducing qualified majority voting (QMV), second by beginning the process of giving the EP more power, and third by making the Internal Market programme possible. Interestingly, rumours circulate that Mrs Thatcher was later reported to have said that if she had known the importance of the SEA, she would have blocked it.

The Common Foreign and Security Policy
Through the latter part of the 1980s, the Cold War drew to an end. The fall of the Berlin Wall in November 1989 was followed by the collapse of communism in East and Central Europe and then in the Soviet Union. The Gulf War in early 1991 proceeded from the Iraqi invasion of Kuwait in August 1990, and was followed by the war in ex-Yugoslavia in June 1991. Basically, the EC faced a situation where they stood on the 'winning side', but under the dominance of the only surviving hegemon, the USA. All these events challenged the EC tremendously. How should Europe organize herself? Which role should Europe play in world affairs, and how should one solve the new German question, that is, ensure that Germany remained within the EC?

During the years following the SEA, the integration process gained momentum, directing the attention to '1992', when the Internal Market would be implemented, allowing for goods, persons, capital and services to move freely within the EC. This process created a mental spillover, paving the road for further integrative steps. Equally it was much the changed situation in the international system which encouraged further integration.

The next stage in the institutional and policy development of the EC and EPC was the intergovernmental conference held at Maastricht in December 1991. The result was the Treaty on European Union. The treaty introduced the 'temple idea', that is, the three pillars: (1) the supranational EC; (2) the not quite intergovernmental common foreign and security policy; and (3) the intergovernmental cooperation on justice and home affairs. The CFSP succeeded the EPC creating several breakthroughs in the old positions.

Summing up, Neil Nugent identifies the six central elements of the CFSP in the Maastricht Treaty as:

(1) the general objectives of the CFSP were identified; (2) systematic co-operation was to be established between the EU States on any matter of foreign and security policy that was of general interest; (3) where it was deemed to be necessary the Council of Ministers should, on the basis of unanimity, define common positions to which the Member states should confirm; (4) on the basis of general guidelines from the European Council, the Council of Ministers could decide that a matter should be subject of a joint action; (5) the CFSP was to include security issues, 'including the eventual framing of a common defence policy, which might in time lead to a common defence'; and (6) the WEU was to be 'an integral part of the development of the Union' (Nugent 1999: 449).

Another important point which ought to have been included in Nugent's list is that the status of the Commission was upgraded. As a direct result it now participates fully in the CFSP (Article J.9), and has the same right as the member states in the European Council to put forward proposals or to call for emergency meetings of the Council (Article J.8). The treaty included the limited possibility of decisions taken by voting; if the European Council should agree on a joint action, the Council of Ministers should be able to vote on the modus of implementing it (Article J.3). The Maastricht Treaty was signed in 1992.

In the Maastricht Treaty it was stipulated that it should be revised in 1996. Thus the Heads of State and Government, together with the Commission, began preparing the next IGC, to the background of the experiences in the Balkans and the possibility of a major Eastern enlargement. It was bad, from an integrationist point of view (a) because there was neither an external nor an internal pressure, or sense of emergency, and (b) there was no time pressure either. The IGC was planned and prepared well in advance, and thus it had time to look into the details and—one might say—of course get stuck in them, which it subsequently did.

The results of the IGC leading to the Amsterdam Treaty have been greatly underestimated mainly because attention was given to the points which it was not possible to solve previously, namely institutional reform, the number of Commissioners, weights of votes and so on. Thus, the achievements were not fully appreciated. In fact the Amsterdam Treaty *inter alia* (1) gave the EP a substantial expansion of power, (2) streamlined the treaty, which was a mess after Maastricht, (3) strengthened the CFSP considerably, and (4) also strengthened the European Council's role as policy-maker.

Belonging to the new elements of the Amsterdam Treaty, mentioned above, was the agreement on the 'constructive abstention' (Article 23). Article 23 stipulates that CFSP decisions as a general rule are taken by unanimity. Should a member state decide not to vote, would that not imply that a decision could not be taken by the others? Should a member state decide not to vote and to make a declaration, that it does so in accordance with this article, then the member state itself is not bound by the decision, but it is not allowed to take actions which would work against the decision of the Council.

As indicated unanimity is the rule, but Article 23.2 states that QMV is to be used when 'by derogation from the provisions of paragraph 1, the Council shall act by qualified majority:

> when adopting joint actions, common positions or taking any other decision on the basis of a common strategy; when adopting any decision implementing a joint action or a common position.

Article 23.2 may sound drastic to people familiar with the EU, but the following text qualifies this by stating that if a member state declares that it intends to vote against a decision, there will be no vote taken. The Council may then decide to let the European Council take a look at the case again, and that could take up to six months before the European Council gathered again. This constructive abstention was a British idea. With only two European Council meetings a year, there was hardly any danger of a decision being taken, as six months in foreign affairs may seem like an eternity; decisions normally have to be taken quickly to have any impact. Thus this principle could be used as an effective veto. The other disadvantages of the constructive abstention are that it shows the outside world that the Union is not united, thus weakening its foreign policy, and the possibility of abuse to avoid participating in the financing of the joint actions.

At least the 'time problem' was solved in October 1998 in the tiny Austrian village Pörtsach, where the Heads of State and Government pragmatically decided to meet as often as necessary. In 1998 the number was four meetings, in 1999 it was six, in 2000 it was four and in 2001 it will remain at this higher level. This frequency of meetings was enough to make the European Council function as some kind of European executive and as the foreign policy dynamo Article 13.1 had foreseen. This article states, that 'The European Council shall define the principles of and general guidelines for the common foreign and security policy, including for matters with defence implications'.

Institutionally, the Amsterdam Treaty brought the creation of a policy unit (Policy Planning and Early Warning Unit), which is an essential tool for conducting a foreign policy. Creating such a unit but placing it under the Council of Ministers, on the one hand, reduced the ultimate dependence on the foreign ministries of the member states. But at the same time, it avoided strengthening the supranational element more than necessary, thus paying respect to the northern European countries' reluctant attitude towards a supranational EU foreign policy. Equally important was the decision that the Secretary General of the Council should also be 'High Representative'. Again, there is a compromise; some integrationist states had preferred a EU Commissioner, or at least some kind of EU foreign minister, whereas others were strictly against this. By giving the job to a civil servant, the inter-governmentalists were calmed, and the EU got a foreign political 'contact' person.

The quantitative jump aimed at in Amsterdam was finally taken when former Spanish Minister and NATO Secretary General Javier Solana was appointed Secretary General of the Council and High Representative. He took office on 18 October 1999. By appointing the NATO Secretary General Solana much of the 'civil servant air' disappeared from the position. Apart from getting a strong political personality, the EU also got one of the few persons, who could at the same time be Secretary General for the Western European Union (WEU), thus strengthening the military dimension of the EU by the 'personal union', and not upsetting the US and the Atlanticist group of the EU member states.

A very important decision was reached at the Helsinki meeting of the foreign ministers in November 1999 and the following confirmation in December by the Heads of State and Government. It was decided to create a 'European military force', with a strength of 60,000 men, to be ready in 2003. The decision was initiated by the St Malo statement of Prime Ministers Jospin and Blair from December 1998 saying, *inter alia,* 'the Union must have the capacity for autonomous action, backed up by credible military forces, the means to decide to use them and a readiness to do so, in order to respond to international crisis'. A lot of words were used to make the decision look like a small, natural development, only centring on the Petersberg tasks (i.e. tasks related to conflict prevention and crisis management under the WEU, but not under NATO). But the nervous US reactions clearly signalled the historical significance of the decision. This was confirmed by the President of the Commission, Prodi, who in an interview in *The Independent*, declared that one could call the force Margrethe or Marianne or something else, but now one had a common defence organization (*Politiken*, 5 February 2000). No matter the name, and the current command structure, the European Union had begun fulfilling what was laid down in Article 17 of the Amsterdam Treaty stipulating the creation of a common defence policy. Thus, what by some commentators and politicians was seen as a few cosmetic changes in Amsterdam, after a few years turned out to be an important strengthening and streamlining of the common European foreign and security policy. Seemingly, only Denmark was afraid of taking the leap, the rest of the countries supported it.

The legacy of the EPC to the CFSP was the economic necessity of a minimum political coordination, which would allow especially the larger member states both to conduct 'their' foreign policy, and look as if the EC stood united. One favourite means was vague and ambiguous statements. The British hoped to transfer this legacy into the EU with the addition to the new way of making foreign political decisions (1996), but in vain. The Pörtsach decision (1998), followed by the Helsinki decisions on European defence and the appointment of Mr Solana to Secretary General of both the Council of Ministers and the WEU (1999) signalled a new era where most member states have agreed on conceiving the EU as their future.

The European Foreign Policy Frameworks

To get an idea of why it is important to look at the foreign policy machinery, let us briefly turn to the discussion of what constitutes a foreign political actor. Gunnar Sjöstedt wrote *the* seminarial work on EC (EU) actorness in 1977. To be an international actor the entity in question must possess two essential qualities: autonomy and actor capability (Sjöstedt 1977: 15-16). Autonomy implies that the unit is discernible from its environment, and that it has a minimal degree of cohesion. Actor capability implies the 'unit's capacity to behave actively and deliberately in relations to other actors in the international system' (1977: 16). To operationalize his definition, Sjöstedt defines a set of variables termed structural prerequisites, grouped in three: (a) basic requirements including a community of interests, a goal articulation system, resource mobilization system and resources for community actions; (b) decision-making and monitoring facilities, including crisis management system, interdependence management system, a normal decision-making system and a control and steering system; and (c) action performance instruments including a network of agents and a network of transaction channels (1977: 74). An important insight of Sjöstedt's is that being an international actor is not the same as being, for example, a superpower.

Actorness is a quality which can vary in strength as is seen when looking at the international system today, with the USA at one end of the continuum and Fiji at the other.[3]

With Sjöstedt in mind, what are the Union's sources of influence? With an area of 3.2 million sq. km and a population of 372 million persons in 1996, the Union is able to compete with the two other large OECD states, the USA (9.3 million sq. km and 261 million inhabitants) and Japan (0.4 million sq. km and 125 million inhabitants). Looking at the EU's wealth, we see that the gross domestic product (GDP) (at market prices current series, Eurostat Yearbook 2000) was 7,593,142 million ECU in 1998, compared to the US's 7,813,767 million ECU and Japan's 3,404,713 million ECU. This implies that the EU's GDP was nearly as large as that of the USA, indicating the huge economic importance of the EU on a world basis. Looking at how the GDP is spent to get an indication of the future, one sees that measured in percentage of domestic GDP, the EU spent 0.76% in 1998 for research and development compared with 0.85% in the USA and 0.62% in Japan. In a competition perspective such figures are worrying as they indicate that the wealth of the EU is by no means secured. Looking at the GDP and R&D the figures indicate something about the potential military power structure (Eurostat Yearbook 2000). With these figures in mind, let us look at the EU's potential military strength.

The combined armed forces of the EU member states in 2000 was approximately 2 million compared with the 1.5 million of the USA. Concerning defence expenditure as a share of GNP, the EU member states on average spent 2% whereas the USA spends around 3% (NATO Review, Summer 2000). Thus one could say that the EU has the potential of counterbalancing the USA, if the EU was able to coordinate its efforts better.

---

3.   Quite a number of scholars have devoted time to the question of how to analyse the EU as an international actor. Among the many important contributions are: Ifestos (1987), Allen and Smith (1990), Hill (1993) and Bretherton and Vogler (1999).

Another element of a state's power resources is the stability of the political system. Although the EU begins to look more and more like a 'real state', the Union, taken as an entity, still constitutes a fragmented political system. This, of course, makes coherent decision-making harder than it already is in a 'normal' European state. This problem is accentuated by the fact that the EU at the beginning of the new millennium consists of 15 states with each having their individual foreign political tradition, and each having their individual perception of what their national interest is. Especially for the old great powers (France, Germany, Italy, Spain and the UK), the process of socializing, and adaptation to a 'common foreign policy' instead of the national one takes time. But, as we shall see, this process of adaptation and compromise has already developed to a surprising extent. We shall return to the question of the EU's actorness at the end of this chapter.

Institutions and Processes[4]

As previously discussed, none of the individual member states can by themselves affect international affairs to a larger extent. The EU brings together 15 highly developed, democratic states in a state-like bloc. This bloc is one of the world's largest economies, and provides more than half of the world's development aid, as well as humanitarian aid. It is these realizations which gradually have created the basis for a EU foreign and security policy.

The EU's foreign and security policy has developed within the two-pillar system (there is no genuine foreign policy issues vested in pillar 3); the supranational within the frame of the EC Treaty and the inter-governmental within the EPC/CFSP framework. The Maastricht Treaty formalized the role of the European Council as superior to both pillars with three direct results: (1) established a new coordinated policy process; (2) decided to make a policy planning unit; and (3) created the foundation for the development of a common defence policy.

The next sections analyse the supranational and the intergovernmental part of the EU's foreign and security policy after the large restructurings which took place in 1999 and 2000. This is to get a systematic overview of the machinery which creates the Union's foreign and security policy in general, and its Middle East policy in particular.

---

4.   Much of the information in this section has been found at the homepage of the Council (http://ue.eu.int/en/summ.htm), and of the Commission (http://europa. eu.int/comm/index_en.htm).

The Supranational Part of the EU's Foreign and Security Policy
The supranational part of the EU's foreign and security policy is the oldest part of its external engagement. Today, foreign policy aspects are found in most Directorate Generals (DGs) demanding much of internal coordination.

The supranational foreign policy of the Union is conducted according to a variety of procedures, sometimes involving the EP more, sometimes less, but always involving the Council of Ministers, which has the final say. This implies that the initiative normally comes from the Commission (a contact from a representation, a suggestion from a lobbyist, an initiative originating in a DG and so on), being prepared in a DG, then coordinated among the cabinets before it is presented in the Commission proper, and eventually sent to the Council of Ministers as an official initiative. From the Council it will be passed on to the Committee of Permanent Representatives known as COREPER with its working groups, before it is presented in the Council of Ministers.

In connection with the supranational part of the EU's foreign and security policy the role of the individual commissioners is important, both as members of the College of Commissioners, that is, the Commission, as personnel responsible for a certain policy, as coordinators of DGs and services, and as heads of DGs. Especially the Commissioner for External Relations is important in this context. This is well illustrated in the 'mission statement' of the External Relations DG:

> The External Relations Commissioner will co-ordinate the external relations activities of the Commission. He will be its interface with the EU's General Affairs Council [i.e., the Foreign Ministers of the Member states], and its interlocutor with the newly-appointed High Representative for the Common Foreign and Security Policy, Mr Javier Solana. The External Relations Commissioner will ensure that the Commission has a clear identity and a coherent approach in its external activities.[5]

The institutional structure of the bureaucracy of the Commission gives a good overview of the Commission's emphasis in the field of international affairs. The central unit is the DG for External Relations, followed by the DG for Enlargement, the DG for Trade and the DG for Development. Adding to these, there are the Common Service for External Relations (SCR), and the European Communities Humanitarian Office (ECHO), both of which are independent units.

---

5.   http://europa.eu.int./comm/dgs/external_relations/general/mission_en.htm

Directorate-General for External Relations
The 'pre-Prodi' structure of external relations reflected the growth of
the external engagement of the Commission. It began with DG I
(Commercial Policy and Relations with North America, the Far East,
Australia and New Zealand), but was extended to DG IA (CFSP,
Europe), and later DG IB (Southern Mediterranean, Middle and Near
East, Latin America and so on). The reform of the Commission initiated
in 1999 has reunited the DG for External Relations to create a coherent
and stronger unit. Today, the DG is responsible for the coordination of
the supranational foreign policy, thus making the Commissioner-in-
charge a very influential person, and interlocutor for the High
Representative of the CFSP. The new structure reflects the growing role
of the EU in international affairs and of the Commission, and it reflects
change from an emphasis on mainly external economic matters to a
position where it plays both a role in foreign policy and foreign
economic policy. Still, its area of responsibility emphasis is foreign
economic relations, including (1) relations to multilateral organizations
such as UN, OSCE, EFTA (but also WEU and NATO); (2) relations to
regions (e.g. Middle East, Asia); (3) bilateral relations to European and
non-European countries (e.g. Russia, USA, China, Japan); and (4) the
administration of the 120 delegations the Commission has around the
world.

Directorate-General for Enlargement
In the Prodi Commission, the Task Force for the Accession Negotiations has been merged with the services responsible for the enlargement
to form a new unit, the DG Enlargement, with Commissioner Günter
Verheugen in charge. The concrete task of this DG is to screen the
applicant countries and draft negotiating positions for the EU member
states.
    The EU began as a group of six countries and has since then grown
to its present size of 15 member states. The special point about this new
process of accession is that apart from Greece, Portugal and Spain, the
other six 'newcomers' (i.e. Austria, Denmark, Finland, Ireland, Sweden
and the UK) were economically and politically on the same level as the
then EC; the new applicants are not. Taught by the problems especially
caused by Greece in its lack of willingness and ability to adapt to its
political culture, the EU has planned the accession process as carefully
as possible this time.

The process was decided upon by the Council of Ministers in 1997. Each applicant is treated as an individual case, and thus accession could be at different times. As accession touches upon both supranational and intergovernmental matters, the Presidency makes negotiation proposals on topics concerning pillars 2 and 3 whereas the Commission, mainly DG Enlargement, makes proposals for points relating to pillar 1. The concrete negotiations are generally conducted by the Permanent Representatives, and the results of the negotiations have to be approved by all member states before they are put together in a draft treaty, which is presented both to the Council of Ministers and the European Parliament for approval.[6]

Directorate-General for Trade
The Common Commercial Policy (CCP) laid down in Article 133 of the Treaty establishing the European Community (TEC) as well as the Common External Tariff (CET) of the EU are some of the Union's oldest and most important external policies. They were already envisaged in the Treaties of Rome and provided the Commission with its prominent role. Today, the EU is the world's largest trading bloc and accounts for approximately 20% of global trade and plays an important role in world economics. Right from the start it was the aim that the EC/EU should speak with one voice when negotiating trade matters with international organizations, or states.

It is possible to group the trade agreements the EU has with third countries into two blocs: trade agreements (Article 133 TEC and sometimes Article 181 TEC on development aspects) and association agreements (Article 310 TEC). The trade agreements include 'trade and economic cooperation agreements' which used to establish a special privileged relationship. Today, the sheer amount of these agreements have eroded their value but they are increasingly tied to conditions on human rights and democracy. Association agreements include preferential treatment as well as the political prospects of close relations to the Union. A special variation are the so-called 'European Agreements' made for Central and Eastern European countries to prepare for their possible EU membership.

The normal decision-making procedure is that the Commission shapes a proposal, which it submits to the Council of Ministers, which sends it to the COREPER. The COREPER sends its submission to the

6.   http://europa.eu.int/comm/enlargenment/negotiations/index.htm

Council of Ministers which either rejects it, or gives the Commission a mandate for negotiating. Simultaneously, with the approval of the Council, it creates an 'Article 133 Committee' which monitors the negotiations conducted by the Commission on behalf of the Union. When the Commission considers negotiations as ended, it presents the result to the Council which either approves, or rejects it. Thus the role of the Commission is very important during the whole process, although member states try to control it. Basically, negotiations on association agreements follow the same path with two differences; first, the EP has to agree to the result of the negotiations, and secondly, the decision on approval in the Council has to be taken by unanimity. These differences signify the political importance of the association agreements in contrast to trade agreements.

Directorate-General for Development

Development cooperation also has a long history in the EU, dating back from the time of the foundation of the European Economic Community, and today the EU is the world's single largest aid donor.

The Maastricht Treaty prioritized development policy clearly, stressing its general principles in Title XX (Articles 177–181 TEC). Article 177 reads:

> 1. Community policy in the sphere of development co-operation, which shall be complementary to the policies pursued by the Member states, shall foster:
> – the sustainable economic and social development of the developing countries, and more particularly the most disadvantaged among them;
> – the smooth and gradual integration of the developing countries into the world economy;
> – the campaign against poverty in the developing countries.

In addition, the next section stipulates the aim of contributing to the consolidation of democracy, rule of law and the respect for human rights.

One should notice that Article 177 TEC states that the development policy of the EU is seen as being *complementary* to that of the member states. This allows the member states to pursue their individual goals and interests reflecting either historical bonds (France, Italy, Portugal, Spain, UK), or normative preferences (Denmark, Ireland, Netherlands). By establishing complementarity as a principle, the states can continue their special relations which, from a collective EU point of view, might be considered questionable.

The reformulation of DG Development policies in 2000 (26 April, IP/00/410) was not in itself dramatic, but it changed the emphasis. The 'reform' of the policy stressed that emphasis should be given to areas:

- that are key aspects of any policy focusing on poverty eradication...
- where the EC has comparative advantages over other donors, either owing to a critical mass...or because of a particular competence...
- for which EU citizens have expressed concern (e.g. democratisation, respect for human rights, support for civil society).
- in which the EU's interests are best served by action at Community level in accordance with the principle of subsidiarity...
- in which, for pragmatic and operational reasons, it is more effective to co-ordinate at European level.[7]

The genuinely 'new' part of the reform concerned the management and coordination of development aid. First, it establishes clearer limits to the tasks of the DG for External Relations and the DG for Development concerning the policy planning and the control of the strategic policy decisions on fund allocations to the various sectors; and secondly, it decided that decisions were to be reached in dialogue with the beneficiary states. The Commission continued:

> This will be combined with the unification of the process involved in managing a project from A to Z, the 'project cycle. 80% of the EU assistance programs...will in future be managed by a new Office within the Commission services, building on the present Common Service for External Relations (SCR). (IP/00/480).

Just as development covers a wide field of subjects, the decision-making processes vary considerably from case to case. If the agreement includes trade or some kind of association, then naturally Articles 133 and 310 TEC are applied as described above, giving the Commission a central role. Other kinds of agreements are handled according to Article 252 TEC which implies that the Commission's initiatives have to pass the Council twice, as well as the EP.

The Common Service for External Relations (SCR)
As a consequence of the extension of the EU's external engagement, the SCR was set up in October 1997, and began operating a year later. Its main task was to coordinate—and control—the supranational part of

---

7.   http://europa.eu.int/comm/dgs/development/mission_en.htm

the Union's aid to third countries, but it soon began engaging in policy-making as well as implementing and controlling. The SCR is an independent unit, but placed under the responsibility of the Commissioner for External Relations, Christopher Patten.

Due to heavy criticism, its future was uncertain until the decision of the Commission of 16 May 2000, to use the SCR as a part of the new project managing reform. The SCR will be transformed into a purely implementing unit, which has to report to a newly created Board of External Relations Commissioners. The chairman of the new board is Christopher Patten and chief executive is Poul Nielson, Commissioner for Development. It is hoped that 'The new entity for managing Community aid will allow the Commission to retain full managerial control over the provisions of external assistance' (IP/00/480).

A frequent criticism has been that the projects were not monitored and often lost focus. The reform foresees a new interdepartmental 'Quality Support Group' that will report to the Board of External Relations Commissioners. 'The group will monitor external assistance programming to ensure that projects meet the Commission's quality standards, policy objectives and priorities. It will also feed evaluations back into the programming system' (IP/00/480).

It is still too early to evaluate the progress made but the division of policy-making, and implementation, as well as the creating of controlling bodies seems sound.

The European Communities' Humanitarian Office
The European Communities' Humanitarian Office (ECHO) was set up in 1992 and is placed under the responsibility of the Commissioner for Development. Its mandate is: 'to provide emergency assistance and relief to the victims of natural disasters or armed conflict outside the European Union'.[8] ECHO may conduct operations on its own, or in cooperation with other organizations, including the UN or states. Apart from fast disaster relief ECHO provides assistance to prevent disasters (e.g. information to affected peoples on landmines, training various specialists). People in ex-Yugoslavia, Caucasus, Rwanda, Burundi and Sudan have all received help.

---

8.   http://europa.eu.int/comm/echo/en/present/manda_en.html

Summing Up

In this section we have taken a look at the supranational part of the EU's foreign and security policy, introducing the overall framework before looking at the single DGs and offices. We saw that most of the supranational part of the EU's foreign and security policy had been reformed, but also that it was still too early to evaluate the results of the reforms. In the next section, we will take a closer look at the intergovernmental part of the foreign and security policy, which has also developed strongly in the last few years, and which constitutes the centre of the EU's CFSP development .

The Intergovernmental Part of the EU's Foreign and Security Policy (CFSP)

Seen schematically, the CFSP institutions resemble that shown in Figure 1.1.

The European Council determines the principles and general guidelines of the European Union's CFSP. The Amsterdam Treaty lists the aims of the CFSP (Article 10 TEU):

> 1. The Union shall define and implement a common Foreign and Security Policy covering all areas of Foreign and Security Policy, the objectives of which shall be:
>
> – to safeguard the common values, fundamental interests, independence and integrity of the Union in conformity with the principles of the United Nations Charter;
> – to strengthen the security of the Union in all ways;
> – to preserve peace and strengthen international security, in accordance with the principles of the United Nations Charter, as well as the principles of the Helsinki Final Act and the objectives of the Paris Charter, including those on external borders;
> – to promote international co-operation;
> – to develop and consolidate democracy and the rule of law, and respect for human rights and fundamental freedoms.

Adding to this the Amsterdam Treaty (Article 17 TEU) gave the European Council the possibility of integrating the WEU fully in the EU and of developing a common defence policy. The members of the European Council are the heads of state and government of the member states. The President of the Commission is fully associated. They are accompanied by the foreign ministers and the Commissioner for External Relations.

Figure 1.1: The CFSP institutions

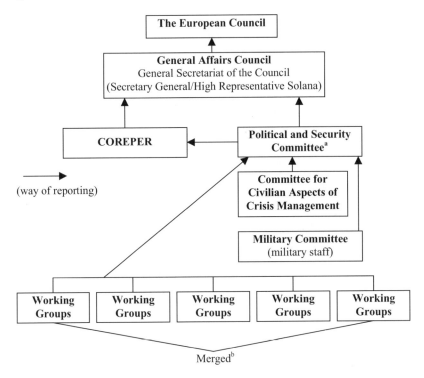

a. May report directly to the GAC on 'affairs arising' prior to Council meetings. Article 25 of the Nice Treaty provides for delegation of powers from the Council in a crisis situation.
b. The COREPER working parties used to consist of Brussels-based diplomats, and the CFSP working parties consisted of diplomats placed in the member state capitals. Now, the two kinds of working parties are merged.

The Council of Ministers consists of ministers from the member states, as well as the relevant Commissioner. The General Affairs Council (GAC) is composed of the foreign ministers. On the basis of the general guidelines received from the European Council, it is responsible for the CFSP on a day-to-day basis, that is, for taking the necessary decisions, controlling the implementation, assuring coherence and effectiveness.

The instruments at the disposal of the CFSP are given in Box 1.1.

Box 1.1: The instruments at the disposal of the CFSP

The treaty lists some of the instruments at the disposal of the EU in its foreign relations; listed hierarchically they are the following:

- A common strategy (Article 13) is the overall approach of the Union towards an important area such as Russia or the Balkans. It is decided by the European Council. It shall 'set out their objectives, duration and the means to be made available by the Union and the Member States'. Common strategies are implemented by joint actions and common positions.
- A joint action (Article 14) is an instrument for implementing a common strategy. 'Joint actions shall address specific situations where operational action by the Union is deemed to be required. They shall lay down their objectives, scope, the means to be made available to the Union, if necessary their duration, and the conditions for their implementation'. When adopting a joint action on the basis of a common strategy the Council does so by QMV.
- A common position (Article 15) is less active than the joint actions. It defines the Union's interests and leaves it up to the member states to act accordingly. Basically, one could consider it as decisive coordination. The text says, 'Common positions shall define the approach of the Union to a particular matter of a geographical or thematic nature. Member States shall ensure that their national policies conform to the common position'. When adopting a common position on the basis of a common strategy the Council does so by QMV.
- The EPC predecessor of the CFSP had as its main instrument, informing and consulting. This is still so for the CFSP now on an obligatory basis (Article 16): 'Member States shall inform and consult one another within the Council on any matter of foreign and security policy of general interest in order to ensure that the Union's influence is exerted as effectively as possible by means of concert and convergent action'.
- The European Council as well as the Council of Ministers also issues declarations and statements on a variety of topics. These are signals on how the EU looks at a specific issue.
- The Union concludes a number of international agreements of very different kinds with third states: trade and association agreements, development agreements, consultation agreements.
- An instrument to signal presence and special importance to an area or a problem is that of the special representatives (Article 18.5) which are sent out by the Council and financed by the Commission. For some years the EU has had a special representative in the Middle East.
- The EU's Reaction Force, as decided at the Helsinki European Council, is an instrument to project power outside the Union. With its planned strength of 50–60,000 men it will have the potential to back up Common Strategies and Joint Actions in a new and more serious way. It will have among its tasks to maintain peace as well as peace making, that is, combat tasks. Apart from these instruments, the traditional diplomatic instruments of dialogue and negotiations belong to the arsenal of the Union.

The President-in-Office changes every six months. The presidency represents the Union in CFSP matters, and is responsible for preparing the necessary proceedings. The presidency is aided by the General Secretariat of the Council of the European Union (i.e. Council of Ministers), the Secretary General of the Council (who is now also High Representative for the CFSP), and when necessary by the Commission. Additionally, the presidency may be assisted by the following presidency, to ensure continuity. The new 'troika' thus consists of four actors: the President-in-Office, the in-coming President-in-Office, the High Representative and a member of the Commission. The presidency is assisted in day-to-day work by the High Representative and the Secretariat General of the Council. The Secretariat General has the 'institutional memory' of the presidency. This is very important as the presidency changes every half year and because each presidency sets its own agenda. This potentially gives the foreign policy of the EU a staccato-like character. The High Representative also plays an important role in this context, as he too can be seen as a guarantee for continuity.

The High Representative is a novel function, and, as such, the conduct of Javier Solana is decisive for its future. As mentioned, the Heads of State and Government chose a political person, and a very active one. This in itself implies that the role of the High Representative is not meant to be that of a traditional civil servant. That Solana looks at it the same way is obvious from the organizational arrangements made by him. The High Representative has delegated most duties not related to foreign policy to the Deputy Secretary General of the Council, thus stressing his prime objective: EU's foreign policy. Apart from his personal cabinet, he has designed the Policy Unit as a form of personal staff, or super-cabinet, which is kept separate from the rest of the Council. The Policy Unit services Solana, who assists the chairman of the Council. It is not the task of the Unit to assist the President-in-Office directly.

The Policy Unit is organized as a very flat pyramid (see Figure 1.2). As the Unit consists of only 23 officers, its organization has been a compromise of various principles (e.g. geographical responsibility, issue-responsibility). It is organized in a number of task forces, each having the responsibility for central parts of the CFSP (policies and strategies) as well as for geographical monitoring. The task force principle implies flexibility. As a matter of principle, task forces can be restructured and changed 'on demand'. Apart from the task forces in general, it is worth drawing attention to two of them in particular. All task forces consist of three persons, apart from the one titled 'European Security and Defence Policy', which has four members, demonstrating the clear priority given this issue by Solana. Equally important is the creation of the Situation Centre which is a crisis management centre. It is still small, but it gives the EU a basic tool to be active and not only reactive in its foreign policy-making. The crisis centre is staffed around the clock, and it is possible to reach it through the telephone number, which Dr Kissinger asked for in the 1970s. Following the terrorist attacks on 11 September 2001, and the wish of the Heads of State and Government to strengthen the CFSP, the Policy Planning Unit expect this to happen.

Figure 1.2: Policy Planning and Early Warning Unit (PPEWU)

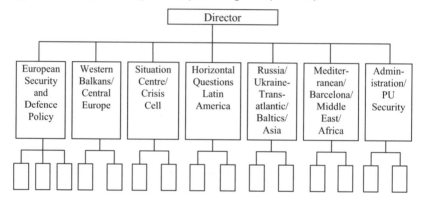

The Committee of Permanent Representatives (COREPER) prepares the agenda of the meetings of the foreign ministers, and is assisted by a number of working parties. The COREPER also includes the submissions of the Political Committee on the agenda, thus having a strong coordinating function. However, the Political Committee, consisting of the political directors of the foreign ministries of the member states, formally has the same rank as the COREPER. *De facto* the COREPER has always been stronger than the Political Committee, as the former meets at least once a week and is permanently in Brussels, while the latter consists of diplomats flying in approximately once a month, thus not having the same networks and permanence.

The Political Committee (see Figure 1.1) is the formal superior to the new Political and Security Political Committee, created in Helsinki.

This new committee is potentially very powerful, as its members are senior ambassadors *and* they stay permanently in Brussels. In turn, they will direct the work of the Military Committee and its military staff, all situated in the same building as the General Secretariat. This new complex of committees clearly signals the importance the CFSP has in the Union.

Friend or Foe? The Cooperation between Council and Commission

The CFSP is still considered the most important and sensitive part of the member states' external roles. History and old bureaucratic traditions have shaped the foreign policies of the individual members, and traditionally, foreign and security policies are seen as the hallmarks of statehood. This is reflected in the division of labour between Commission and Council. Roughly speaking, high politics (traditional foreign policy) lie with the Council, low politics (e.g. trade policy) within the Commission's framework. There is nothing indicating that the Commission will gain more foreign political competencies. For a while it seemed as if the Commission accepted this situation and instead was helping to develop the foreign and security policy of the Union, under the auspices of the Council and especially the High Representative. However, Mr Prodi's speech to the European Parliament on 3 October 2000 signalled an unwillingness to accept the *status quo*. He pleaded for moving Solana's cabinet and competencies to the Commission. Still, the Commission is in a weak position, should a power struggle break out between the Commission and the Council of Ministers.

This institutional structure can clearly create problems of coordination and institutional rivalries. The Commission had, on various occasions, been criticized heavily for its lack of internal coordination (e.g. SOU 1996: 6). Thus, the new Prodi Commission started to restructure the External Relations Directorates General, creating one new entity instead of the three old DGs and giving the Commissioner for External Relations, Christopher Patten, the overall responsibility for the internal coordination of the Commission's external relations policies. Basically, coordination takes place (or could take place) at several levels. The Commission is represented in the European Council by its President; the relevant Commissioner participates in the foreign ministers' Council, and the Commission is represented in the relevant working parties. The problem of coordination does not lie in the coordination between Council and Commission, but more in the internal coordination of the Commission. This problem was, as mentioned, recognized by the Prodi Commission.

With the central position of the Commissioner for External Relations, the cooperation between Commissioner Patten and Secretary General Solana has become essential. The overall assessment is that this works well both on the professional and the personal level.

The new approach does not conceal the fact that there are still occasional rivalries between the bureaucracies of the Council and the Commission at the lower levels. An example illustrates this; as the Heads of State and Government decided to send Solana and Verheugen, Enlargement Commissioner, to Turkey in 2000, it caused fury in parts of the Commission bureaucracy that Solana appeared in the media as the main person. Those in the Commission felt that they had made all the preparatory work, and that Solana got all the credit. Still, the overall pattern is one of cooperation rather than rivalry in day-to-day work.[9] This is paramount if the EU is going to play an active foreign political role.

Coordination within the Commission and between the Commission and the Council of Ministers is only one aspect of the coordination problem. Equally large is the issues of coordination among the 15 member states. The whole history of the EPC and the CFSP can be seen as one long process of learning and adaptation; learning that individual European states no longer are able to shape and influence the international system as they could until the Second World War, although some states tried it anyway (e.g. Suez 1956). Member states have had to adapt to, or get used to cooperating on the most sacred of all things, national foreign policy. The member states had to adjust to not only looking at some kind of narrowly defined 'national interest' but also looking at the interests of the EU *per se*, and not only as an instrument to pursue own interests. This process has, of course been hardest for the great powers, and is not yet finished, if it ever will be. Still, signs of the progressing 'we-feeling' are seen in, *inter alia*: Article 11.2 TEU stating that 'The Member states shall support the Union's external and security policy actively and unreservedly in a spirit of loyalty and mutual solidarity... They shall refrain from any action which is contrary to the interests of the Union or likely to impair its effectiveness as

9.   An example is the praise by Commissioner Patten of the work of the Policy Unit in his speech of 22 February 2000.

a cohesive force in international relations'; Article 19.1 TEU stating that 'In international organisations and at international conferences where not all the Member states participate, those which do take part shall uphold the common positions'; and Article 20 TEU on the need for diplomatic and commission delegations to cooperate and work together.

Apart from official coordination among the member states within the framework of the Council of Ministers , it also takes place in other, less open forms. The Benelux states used to coordinate their approaches before important meetings, but seemingly this coordination is decreasing in intensity. This cannot be said about the number of great power consultations; the most powerful is no doubt the Paris–Berlin axis which was institutionalized by the 1963 Elysée Treaty. Most important EU initiatives over the years either came from this partnership directly, or have been cleared there before being launched. Another less strong axis is London–Paris, of which one offspring was the St Malo declaration on a Common European Defence. A less known, but powerful and very unofficial institution, is the so-called '*quint*'. It consists of Germany, France, Italy, Spain and the UK. It is not formalized with regular meetings—as far as is known—but it meets ad hoc, to coordinate and consult among the great powers of the EU. The meetings take place at either ambassadorial or ministerial level. It is, not surprisingly, regarded with strong suspicion by the smaller member states, although there is a certain understanding of its existence out of pure efficiency considerations. The interests of the five quint states are perceived as being so different that they do not, at the moment, pose a genuine threat to the official procedures in the Council of Ministers.

Coordination problems are very real and always have to be taken into consideration when judging the quality of the EU's performance as an international actor. When this is done one has to accept that the results achieved are reasonably good, but it will take some kind of international crisis or major negotiation to show how the new system really works under pressure.

The Foreign Policy of the European Union

Intuitively, the EU is easily accepted as a foreign political actor; its mere presence has created expectations among the other actors of the international community. Expectations that often have not been met in the past have created frustrations. Most states in the world have missions accredited to the EU in Brussels, and the EU has led other states to act differently than they otherwise would have done. Thus, the Union 'makes a difference' in foreign policy. Here it would be worth recalling Sjöstedt's already mentioned insight, that being an international actor is a quality which can vary in intensity. Today the EU possesses all the prerequisites Sjöstedt mentioned in 1977 to be an international actor. Thus, the question is the degree to which the EU is an international actor. The EU's new CFSP structure after Maastricht, Amsterdam and Helsinki has given it the dynamism and instruments which were needed to talk of a genuine European foreign and security policy. It would now be hard to deny that the European Union has its own foreign and security policy. The EU's foreign and security policy is not as developed and as coherent as that of a traditional nation state often is. Perhaps the best picture is to describe it as an adolescent, with all that implies. But the '11 September' has had a maturing impact on the EU in general including the CFSP. It is the widespread feeling in the European capitals that the EU needs to strengthen itself to be able to act as a credible actor.

In trying to describe the nature of the EU's foreign policy, it can be characterized as 'confederated'. There are foreign policy tasks taken care of by the individual member states and foreign policy tasks undertaken by the EU as such. The states decide, each with a veto right, whether to hand over foreign-political competencies to the Commission, to the Council, or not at all. This model partly resembles the Swiss confederation in the seventeenth century. Seen from an economic, or efficiency point of view, this could be considered a sub-optimal solution, as all 15 member states have to keep diplomatic services which on the whole perform the same tasks, thus 'wasting' a lot of resources and demanding much effort in coordinating the 15 points of view. From a political and also an emotional point of view, this construction makes good sense; foreign policy is, as said, the hallmark of statehood, and, thus only likely to disappear as the last of competencies are handed over to the EU.

2 |

Approaching the Middle East*

Europe and the Ottoman Empire during the Nineteenth Century

The main focus of this book is the Arab Middle East. In order to provide a more precise picture of the historical developments in the region, however, it will for a moment be necessary to go back on our initial definition of 'the Middle East'. The purpose of this chapter is first to provide an overview of the Ottoman Empire and its Arab provinces, and then show how the Middle East as we know it today was formed out of the ruins of the Ottoman Empire. It will also explain why during the world wars the European powers and, later during the Cold War, the superpowers sought control over the region.

At the beginning of the nineteenth century the Ottoman Empire consisted of the countries (apart from its European provinces) in the region today known as Tunisia, Algeria, Libya, Egypt, Jordan, Israel/Palestine, Lebanon, Syria, Yemen, Iraq, and Saudi Arabia. The area was divided into provinces that were controlled by a governor who owed ultimate allegiance to Istanbul (Owen 1992: 8).

The invasion and occupation of Egypt in 1798 by France marked the beginning of the inter-European rivalry over the Arab Provinces of the Ottoman Empire as well as the first serious geopolitical loss for the Ottoman Empire in more recent times. Egypt was important because of its geo-strategic position in the Middle East as the passageway to Asia and Africa. For the European empires, access to their dominions farther afield was a vital interest. The French invasion was thus inspired by a desire to threaten British access to India and other parts of the Far East. Great Britain was indeed concerned, but remained more focused on limiting Russian influence in the region, for this could prove a more serious threat to British interests.

---

* We would like to thank Jean Monnet Professor Henrik Plaschke for his comments on this chapter.

In 1802, the French forces in Egypt attempted an invasion of Syria, which was resisted by a military alliance between Britain and the Ottomans leading to France losing both Syria and Egypt. Mohammad Ali, an emissary of Sultan Mahmud, then seized power in Egypt and over a generation he managed to turn Egypt into a larger Mediterranean power by initiating a small scale revolution in fields such as infrastructure, technology, education and not least the military (Findlay 1994: 27). A new situation then began to emerge. During the early 1830s Mohammad Ali expanded his sphere of influence to Syria and Palestine. His forces even proceeded as far as Istanbul where an overthrow of the sultan, and with him the Empire, was considered (Mansfield 1992: 108). As all other options failed, Sultan Mahmud appealed to Russia who provided military support, but as a *quid pro quo* forced him to sign the Treaty of Hunkiar Iskelessi in 1833. The treaty granted Russia the right to intervene in Turkish affairs and a secret clause permitted 'Russia to insist on the closing of the Dardanelles in time of war' (Mansfield 1992: 108). The sultan was now under pressure from Russia on the eastern front and Mohammad Ali in the south. The sultan decided to attack Mohammad Ali, but was soundly defeated. Mohammad Ali continued the expansion of his sphere (which both formed modern Saudi Arabia) of influence and by the late 1830s, Mohammad Ali controlled Egypt, Syria, the Nedj, Hejaz and even parts of Yemen.

By now the UK also was troubled by Mohammad Ali's increasingly powerful position, which had the potential to affect the UK's interests in the region. The UK became determined to curb Mohammad Ali's ambitions and also to ensure the territorial integrity of the Ottoman Empire. In 1839, the UK occupied Aden to provide a point on an alternative deep ocean route to India, and over the following years the UK strengthened its position in the Gulf, Arabia and Persia. In sum, access to or control of the lines of communication and transport in the Middle East remained a primary objective for the UK as well as other European powers, such as France and Russia. With the 1841 Treaty of London, an international alliance against Mohammad Ali saw that Syria was formally returned to the sultan and the Egyptian army was cut to 18,000 troops. Mohammad Ali was made hereditary viceroy of Egypt and promised not to threaten the Ottoman sultan again.

European Trade and Economic Relations with the Ottoman Empire
In addition to the geo-political interests, a major driving force behind the expansion of the European empires both in relation to the Ottoman

Empire and elsewhere was European industrialization. This led to an increased demand for raw materials, such as cotton and rubber, which were only obtainable from countries with warmer climates. Furthermore, as the domestic markets were satiated there was an increased demand for new outlets for the outpouring of cheap manufactured goods.

Also, the accumulation of wealth strengthened European interests in international lending and investment and during the latter part of the nineteenth century the modernization of many parts of the Ottoman Empire was financed by loans from Europe. Economic concessions were usually granted on unfavourable terms and guaranteed by European states, especially the UK and France, who reserved the right of intervention in case of default (Weiss and Green 1988: 272). As the servicing of interests and repayments became impossible due to absent revenues or mismanagement, it was the European state creditors who took control of finance and public debt and thus gradually came to manage the domestic financial affairs of the Ottoman Empire.

Another point worth mentioning is the fact that trading with the Ottoman Empire was complicated because of different monopolies. In order to advance its commercial relations with the Ottoman Empire, the UK took advantage of Sultan Mahmud's waning influence during the 1830s and coerced him to sign the Anglo-Turkish Commercial Convention of 1838. The treaty is an important example of concessions which included 'exemption from the jurisdiction of Islamic laws and from Ottoman taxes along with fixed low customs duties on imports and exports' (Weiss and Green 1988: 273).

Egypt: Bankruptcy and Invasion
The Khedive Ismail, who ruled Egypt between 1862 and 1879, was often described as a visionary entrepreneur, untroubled by any finer grasp of economy (Hourani 1994: 309-10). The American Civil War benefited Egyptian cotton export and helped finance infrastructural projects, such as railways and irrigation systems. After the end of the war, as exports declined, Ismail took up borrowing in Europe to 'keep up the pace'. He signed an extremely unfavourable concession for the building of the Suez Canal, which was vetoed by the Ottoman sultan. The Commission of Arbitration forced Egypt to pay a hefty compensation, which further damaged Egypt's already strained economy.

In spite of some progress in trade exports and development, the success was mainly based on loans, and in 1876 Egypt defaulted. The

Council of Public Debt ensured France's and Britain's shared control of Egypt's finances and the interests of their respective bondholders. However, Egyptian landowners and military became increasingly opposed to the European control over the country and in 1881 a group of officers led by Colonel Urabi seized power in Egypt.

France and Britain refused to recognize Urabi's government. Eventually, in 1882, Britain invaded Egypt with the main objective of restoring fiscal prudence and, more implicitly, British control of the Suez Canal. At the same time as part of the rivalry between the European empires it became something of a balancing act to avoid war with France which was concerned about British control of both the Nile and the Canal. Although Egypt under the British occupation officially remained a nominally autonomous viceroyalty of the Ottoman Empire under the suzerainty of the sultan, power remained firmly in the hands of the British until 1956 (Skovgaard-Petersen 1995: 55).

Syria and Palestine
In Syria, Ibrahim Pasha established the foundation for a strong state and a self-sustaining economy by developing an educational system, a tax system and a governmental administration. In his efforts to strengthen equality between Muslims and non-Muslims he gradually introduced a secularization of society including a secular courts system that eventually came to challenge the authority of the *Sharia*, Islamic law, and the power of the *ulama*, the religious scholars (Armstrong 1998: 322; Skovgaard-Petersen 1995: 57).

In Palestine, and especially in Jerusalem, religious groups took advantage of their position in 'the Holy City'. This was encouraged by the European powers who, when acting as religious protectors or sponsors, gained political and diplomatic influence through the consulates and churches (Armstrong 1998: 323-25). As an example of the religious sponsorship, in 1860 a Syrian civil war led to massacres of Christians living in Mount Lebanon. Supported by the major European powers France intervened and created a *sanjak*, or privileged district, in Lebanon detached from Damascus.

Maghreb
Turning to the North African provinces of the Ottoman Empire, a further blow to the Ottoman Empire came with the French invasion of Algiers in 1830. With piracy in the Mediterranean Sea, the official

reason was that French merchants needed a secure trading post on the coast of North Africa. However, Algiers was soon annexed by France and the country later experienced a very strong case of European colonization (Mansfield 1992: 117).

Independent Tunisia faced similar financial problems. In 1869 the country was managed by an international commission and in 1881 France occupied Tunisia and made it a protectorate (Mansfield 1992: 110-11). In 1860 Spain invaded Morocco to gain control of Ceuta and Melilla and to limit British influence in the area. Italy had become more interested in North Africa, but it was not until 1911 that she made her mark with the occupation of Tripoli and Libya (Hourani 1994: 311-12).

The Arab Provinces and the Tanzimat
During the nineteenth century the Ottoman Empire lost most of its European provinces. During the early part of the nineteenth century Britain,

> encouraged Ottoman officials to undertake administrative and legal reforms...in the hope of stabilizing the regime and forestalling further European inroads. But Ottoman efforts, though relatively successful, were hampered by internal opposition and rising nationalist sentiments that fostered separatist movements backed by European nations (Smith 1992: 14).[1]

A rebellion in Greece, ironically aided by Anglo-Russian intervention, ultimately resulted in Greek independence in 1833 (Hourani 1994: 296). Later, an important point was the Conference of Berlin in 1878, organized in the wake of the 1877–78 Russo-Turkish War. Montenegro, Romania and Serbia were granted independence, and Bosnia-Herzegovina came under the control of Austria (Smith 1992: 14). With the loss of the European provinces Istanbul began to focus increasingly on the Arabian Peninsula. The Hejaz was the most important Arab province because of the two holy places, Mecca and Medina, which still provided some legitimacy for the ruler of an Islamic state. Sultan Abdul Hamid II was thus eager to ensure the loyalty of his Arab subjects and did so by promoting pan-Islamism and other religious work. Still, the ultimate control of the Hejaz was in the hands of the Grand Shariff of Mecca, Hussein Bin Ali.

---

1.   This can be seen as one of the many actions conducted by European powers, which helped to undermine the Ottoman Empire.

By 1913, a new leader in the central parts of the Arabian Peninsula Abdul Aziz Ibn Saud had in an alliance with the Islamic puritans, the Wahhabis, gained control of Riyadh and al-Hasa and was soon recognized as 'the Sultan of the Nejd and its Dependencies' (Mansfield 1991: 131). Britain had established hegemony over the Gulf and controlled the foreign relations of the coastal sheikhdoms such as Kuwait, Bahrain and Qatar, which served as buffers for potential Ottoman or other European invasions (Mansfield 1991: 121).

The *Tanzimat* introduced in 1839 was a series of reforms that signalled a modernization of the society and a break with the past. In brief, the *Tanzimat* led to a gradual secularization of the Ottoman Empire where citizens were to be equal under the law regardless of race and creed. State-funded secular schools and universities were introduced and military education was modernized, that is Westernized. Nevertheless, finance remained the primary obstacle to implementation of reforms and soon there seemed to be no alternative to international borrowing for Istanbul and it was this situation that paved the way for European influence over Ottoman finances.

Opposition: The Young Ottoman Turks
As a result of the *Tanzimat*, the emerging educated middle class was growing frustrated with the autocratic sultan, and the gradual losses of the European provinces and events in Mount Lebanon were perceived as humiliations of the Ottoman elite, fuelling opposition. The Committee of Union and Progress (CUP) was a clandestine opposition movement set up in 1895 by reformist intellectuals who were joined by a group of military officers in 1906. In 1908, the CUP seized power and returned the country to constitutional rule, which included elections to a new parliament. As tensions between Ottoman liberalism, which advocated equality between Muslims and non-Muslims, and Turkish nationalism increased during the following year, the CUP advocated Turkish nationalism/pan-Turkism and centralization of power. The cultural 'turkification' of the Arab lands was resented, but the opposition was cultural rather than political and social, and therefore the Ottoman rule over Arab lands as such was largely unchallenged (Mansfield 1992: 160).

As World War I was approaching, the CUP leadership failed to secure an alliance with Russia, Britain and France, but turned instead to Germany and the Austrian-Hungarian Empire. Britain declared war on

Germany on 4 August 1914, and even though the leadership made several attempts to avoid the conflict, the Ottoman Empire declared war on the Allies on 5 November 1914.

Summing up, in spite of attempts at reform, the Ottoman Empire lacked the ability to create a counterbalance to European influence, which was becoming increasingly powerful in fields such as industry and military technology. The Ottoman Empire was further weakened by lacking advances in infrastructure such as lines of communication and transport. Also, gradual secularization created further turbulence within society. From an international perspective, the European powers had (at least until 1870) supported the territorial integrity of the Ottoman Empire as a buffer against Russian politico-strategic influence in the region as well as against Russian excursions into Europe proper. Britain's relationship to Russia improved in the early twentieth century and the Ottoman Empire ceased to be a vital interest for Britain. Thus the interests of the European powers vis-à-vis the Ottoman Empire altered from support of the territorial integrity to a fight for the gains of a partition in the aftermath of World War I.

World War I and the Inter-war Years

At the beginning of the war, the Allies and particularly Britain feared a call for a *jihad*, holy war, as the reaction of the Muslim population, especially in India, would be unpredictable. Istanbul made the call immediately, but to take full effect it had to be endorsed by the Grand Shariff of Mecca. The Hashemite Shariff, Hussein Bin Ali was faced with the dilemma of whether to make the call which Istanbul strongly advocated and thus choose the Turkish-German alliance, or instead mount an Arab revolt against the Ottoman Empire which Britain and France wanted. Hussein's primary objective was to secure support for Arab independence in the Provinces after the war.

At first his strategy was to sound out the two sides. As the British appeared supportive of Hussein's demands, he began corresponding with the British High Commissioner in Cairo, Henry McMahon between July 1915 and January 1916. In the so-called Hussein–McMahon correspondence Hussein bargained with Britain over the Arab conditions for joining the war. The outcome of the negotiation was that in return for a revolt against the Ottomans Britain promised independence for the Arab Provinces (Findlay 1994: 35). However,

Britain made a series of reservations most importantly regarding areas 'not purely' Arab, that is, the area west of the districts of Aleppo, Hama, Homs and Damascus, and regarding the protection of French interests in the area. Hussein was not content with the British offer, but apparently saw no alternative than to side with the British, mainly because Turkish troops were at that time heading for the Hejaz and would soon be able to threaten Hussein's position. Therefore, on 10 June 1916, Hussein started what has been described as the Arab Revolt, where he conquered and consolidated his power over the Hejaz and helped the British in gaining the Fertile Crescent.

Simultaneously, in 1916 Britain, France and Russia concluded a secret deal on the postwar partition of the Arab Provinces after World War I—the Sykes–Picot Agreement. The agreement divided the area into five parts:

> (1) The Levant coast which the French claimed, (2) the Syrian hinterland which the French would assist [the word used is *soutenir*]; (3) a zone in Palestine which would be internationalized; (4) British protected areas of Transjordan and much of Iraq; and (5) British-controlled area of Baghdad and the Basra (Polk 1991: 100).

The agreement was essentially a wartime collusion, which was changed in 1918 and the plans ignored the agreements made with Hussein. Although Hussein was getting wind of the agreement, it was not until 1917 that the new Russian government published it. Hussein was not impressed but he was by then too dependent on British aid to change his policies.

The Balfour Declaration and the Zionist Movement
Another crucial event was the release of the Balfour Declaration of 2 November 1917, where the British government officially declared support of 'the establishment in Palestine of a national home for the Jewish people' and 'nothing shall be done which may prejudice the civil and religious rights of existing non-Jewish communities in Palestine' (Laqueur and Rubin 1995, The Balfour Declaration). The declaration was a result of several factors. The drive for a Jewish homeland/state had gathered momentum during the 1890s. Theodore Herzl saw the creation of a Jewish state as a solution to the anti-Semitism and the lack of assimilation of Jews in Europe and with the establishment of the World Zionist Organization in 1897, diplomatic efforts to achieve a Jewish homeland/state were intensified. After con-

sidering different options in Africa and South America from 1914 the World Zionist Organization focused solely on Palestine where Jewish immigration had increased between 1904 and 1914 (Massalha 1994: 123).

Britain saw several advantages in declaring its commitment to the Zionist aspirations. First, in the ongoing war where the Allies were pressed, Britain hoped to encourage American Jewry to pressure the US government to enter the war and Russian Jewry, believed to be influential in the new Bolshevik government, to let Russia remain in the war. Secondly, regarding Britain's imperial and strategic interests it was then believed that a Palestine for the Jews under British and *not* international control would be preferable. Thirdly, on the domestic scene, the intense lobbying by leading British Zionists paid off (Smith 1992: 50).

The Formation of the Modern Middle East

The end of World War I meant the end of the Ottoman Empire. In 1918, Britain controlled Egypt, Palestine, Syria and Iraq whereas France still maintained her claim to Syria. In December 1918, the Sykes–Picot Agreement was revised and in May 1920, at the San Remo Conference, the League of Nations confirmed Britain as mandatory power over Palestine; France over Syria and Lebanon; and endorsed the Balfour Declaration, which was to be implemented by Britain. Soon after, Arab opposition to the British occupation intensified and became rather costly to the British because of military interventions. Domestically, the financial constraints eventually forced the British government to reconsider its involvement in the region, and thus the purpose of the Cairo Conference of 1921 was to reduce the costs of maintaining the mandates.

The New States

An overview of the new states exhibits some of the problems they were facing. Iraq gained independence in 1930, but foreign policy was still to be coordinated with London. Iraq joined the League of Nations in 1932. Still, constant tensions between the king and the parliament led to a military coup in 1936 which was supported by a reformist middle class and nationalist army officers (Yapp 1996: 70-77). The creation of most states in the Middle East—including Iraq—was done with little attention to religious and ethnic groupings. This necessitated the presence of a strong military, which absorbed resources that could have been used on social development instead. Oil was exploited in commercial quantities from the 1930s onwards and made Iraq the second major oil producer in the region at that time.

In Syria and Lebanon, French interests were mainly guided by expected economic advantages, but focused also on 'civilizing' missions and educational activities. Throughout the mandatory period French rule was troubled by rebellions, the most notable being that of 1925–27 which began as tensions between the administration and the Druze community spread to most parts of Syria. During the 1930s several unsuccessful attempts were made at constitutional rule. In 1940 a Vichy high commissioner was installed. Fearing the influence of the Axis-powers, Britain and Free France invaded in 1941 and as tensions between the Free French rulers and nationalists intensified, France eventually pulled out in 1946 giving Syria independence (Maoz and Yaniv 1986: 10).

The Lebanese Republic was established in 1926 and its parliamentary system was based on confessional rule based on the size of the religious groupings where the president was Maronite Christian, the prime minister was Sunni Muslim, and the president of the Chamber of Deputies was Shii Muslim. However, the last public census was conducted in 1932 and Lebanon's population can safely be assumed to have changed since, but any such measure would be too explosive politically and otherwise (Findlay 1994: 13-15). In 1944 France gradually handed over power to the Lebanese parliament and final independence was gained in 1945. In spite of the unpopularity of the French rule improvements were made in areas such as administration, education and land registration (Yapp 1994: 108).

In Arabia, Abd Al-Aziz Al-Saud became king of the newly formed Saudi Arabia in 1932. The new state was very poor, mainly with desert and only a few oases, which could support agriculture. Nevertheless, Saud managed to establish control over the tribes and integrate the different regions into a political unit (Polk 1991: 146). With independence in 1932, the main concern of Saud was poverty. The main sources of revenue were the Mecca pilgrims and the potential Western investments and oil supplemented by the religious donations, the *Zakat*. As ruler, Saud was unchallenged, although the Islamic puritans, the Wahhabis criticized the increasing Western influence. Nevertheless,

Saud granted oil concessions to Standard Oil of California in 1933 (renamed Arabian-American Oil Company, ARAMCO, in 1944) which found oil in the late 1930s. Efficient exploitation was prevented by the onset of World War II—a problem other oil states were also exposed to. In Saudi Arabia, oil revenues became the primary factor in the social development and promotion of education, and 'in bringing about the abandonment of nomadism and facilitating the process of settlement' (Yapp 1996: 192).

The Gulf states were still under the control of Great Britain. However, in Kuwait the Emir granted a concession to the Kuwait Oil Company and American Gulf Oil Company, and oil was found in 1938. In Bahrain oil was found in 1932 but only fully exploited after World War II. Bahrain was one of the first to increase public spending on social services and education. After World War I, the borders of the Gulf states were only loosely defined, but as oil and other subsoil materials were found there was an intensified need to agree to borders, if nothing else to delineate the areas of the concessions.

Egypt remained unstable from 1922 until her formal independence in 1936. The monarch, the parliament and the British were the three main actors engaged in a constant power struggle where Britain still had the upper hand because of control of the ministries of war, justice and finance. The Anglo-Egyptian Treaty of 1936 secured Egypt's independence, but Britain maintained a military presence in the Suez zone and in the Sinai, as well as an unrestricted right to the use of Egyptian territory in case of war. The opposition to British presence inspired nationalism and the creation of the Muslim Brotherhood, which was an opposition to secular nationalism and the European influence (Skovgaard-Petersen 1995: 72). Furthermore, education was improved and the military colleges opened to lower classes.

Transjordan was made independent in 1928, although Britain maintained control of foreign affairs and finance. King Abdullah had some success in the consolidation of his new state where he managed to quell resistance from the tribes in the south, and with the newly founded Arab Legion protect the south and eastern borders. He was also ambitious and never gave up the hope of seeing himself as king of a Greater Syria incorporating Palestine and Syria, led from Damascus.

Palestine was relatively quiet between 1921 and 1929 (Massalha 1994: 128-29). During the same period attempts at creating a national representative council was boycotted by the Arabs because it would be interpreted as an indirect recognition of the Jewish claims. The Wailing Wall riots in 1929 ended the peace and with Jewish immigration in 1931–35 the situation deteriorated even further. The Jewish immigrants were supported by European funding. Between 1936 and 1939 there were rebellions and strikes and the violence between the two groups intensified. Attempts were made at prohibiting Palestinian access to arms, while the Zionists received weapons from Europe (Massahla 1994: 129-30). The British White Paper in 1939, which advocated an independent Palestinian state and limitations on Jewish immigration, calmed the situation somewhat in Palestine. Everyone awaited the outcome of the coming war.

World War II and After

In 1940, Italy began to threaten British positions in Northern Africa and the German invasions of Yugoslavia and Greece opened the possibility for an invasion of Syria and Lebanon. However, this was countered by the occupation of Syria and Iraq by the forces of Free France and Britain. In 1941, Germany invaded the USSR which then elicited a British and Soviet occupation of Iran. In 1942–43, the Italian forces in Egypt and other parts of Northern Africa received support from German forces. This resulted in an Anglo-American intervention which forced the German-Italian forces to withdraw from the region and this event essentially marked the end of World War II in the Middle East and Northern Africa (Hourani 1994: 382-84).

Until now we have been using the term 'the Middle East'. Some would argue that the correct term would have been 'the Near East' stressing the relation to the Ottoman Empire. From a historical point of view, however, Yapp argues that 'the Second World War marks the period when the old concept of the Middle East with its core in the former Ottoman territories gives way to a new concept of a Middle East with its heartland in the Arab world' (Yapp 1996: 390).

The International System Post-World War II

After the war the two major powers present in the Middle East were Britain and the Soviet Union. France remained a mandatory power but its influence had been considerably weakened by the German wartime occupation and the main national efforts were then focused on re-establishing the country. The Soviet Union attempted to establish a stronger presence in the northern states bordering the USSR, the so-called 'Northern Tier', that is, Turkey and Iran. The Soviet goal was to establish a defensive zone of buffer states in the Middle East, similar to Eastern Europe. But the efforts failed and instead the Soviets managed to drive these states to seek a closer alliance with the West. Relations remained tense until 1953 (Yapp 1996: 397).

Great Britain was by far the most dominant power in the region after the war. Britain had established a sphere of influence in the southern Middle East and controlled the Gulf, south-west Arabia and the Sudan. This British sphere stretched from the Mediterranean Sea to the Gulf, and the landlocked areas opened the possibility for transport lines, such as air corridors. In an attempt to consolidate her interests further Britain proposed the establishment of a military confederacy and an economic development programme where Egypt as a state was to have been the central element. The purpose was twofold, namely to protect British interests in the region, oil and communication, and to create a Middle Eastern 'shield' for the protection of Africa (Yapp 1996: 397). Embarrassingly, Britain failed to reach an agreement with Egypt, which weakened its position in relation to the negotiations with other countries. This came to view when Britain signed a treaty with Iraq in 1947, which was abrogated by the Iraqis already in 1948 after riots in Baghdad. Relations to Transjordan were more positive. The Anglo-Jordanian Treaty of 1947 gave Transjordan limited independence, but still allowed a British military presence in the country.

So, in spite of its strength in the region, the British position was thus not unchallenged. On the one hand domestic factors, such as the economy, were soon to force Britain to subject the Empire to review and on the other, after the war the US and the USSR were established as the two key actors in international politics. With Britain's dependence on US financial support the power of the British Empire was on the wane.

Palestine and the Israeli–Arab War of 1948–49
During the mandatory period the British had made several attempts at establishing some kind of joint self-autonomy institutions for the Palestine Arabs and the Zionists, but to no avail. At the end of World War II, supported by the British, the Zionists established para-statal institutions and military groups. The Palestinian Arabs were far less organized and troubled by internal rivalries (Massalha 1994: 128). As

relations between Palestine Arabs and the Jewish immigrants deteriorated rapidly, the British presence attempted to keep the two parties apart and prevent direct-armed confrontations. From a British perspective, the situation was complicated further by the state of the British economy, which had been strained during the course of the war so expenses related to the mandates had to be cut. This was done by troop withdrawals leaving the British Royal Air Force as the dominant military presence. With the violence and constant tensions, by 'September 1947 Palestine was seen to be an economic and strategic liability and Britain's problem one of damage limitation' (Yapp 1996: 399). Consequently, the British decided to leave Palestine.

The Partition Plan for Palestine, formulated and recommended by the United Nations Special Committee on Palestine, was passed by the UN on 27 November 1947. It was met with Arab outrage and a muted Jewish reception. Shortly after the Partition Plan was announced, Britain declared that the British mandatory administration of Palestine would be ending by 15 May 1948. On that same day the Zionists in Palestine proclaimed the state of Israel while refraining from defining the territorial borders of the new state. The rationale was not to define any geographical area as the war, which everybody expected to be imminent, could alter the situation.

War

The Arab world's military response to the Israeli declaration of independence has often been heavily criticized. However, it is important to be aware of the domestic situation in the states bordering Palestine on the eve of the war. When the war broke out, Egypt, Syria and Iraq were facing mounting internal instability, which eventually led to revolutions during the 1950s. Therefore, it was a question of first safeguarding domestic stability and security and then nurturing the reputation as Arab nationalists (Salibi 1998: 156-58).

In Jordan, however, King Abdullah had, contrary to all expectations, full control over the country and was quite capable of dispatching the Arab Legion, but unwilling to enter Palestine without a clear mandate from the newly formed Arab League or an invitation from the Palestinian Arabs. However, after lengthy discussions in May 1947 troops from several Arab states finally intervened in Palestine without coordination, strategy or goal, and were rather unsurprisingly soundly defeated. Subsequently, King Abdullah assumed leadership over the Arab involvement in Palestine, but the task was far from easy. The Jewish forces numbered about 74,000 to the 7500 of the Arab Legion and they were equipped with more sophisticated weaponry. The war wound down between February and July 1949, not by the signing of one multilateral peace treaty, but rather by a series of armistice agreements (Yapp 1996: 139). At the end of the war, the West Bank and the Arab Quarters of Jerusalem were under Jordan's control. Egypt controlled Gaza. Approximately 700,000 Palestinian Arabs were expelled or fled, some to the Jordanian East Bank, some farther afield (Smith 1992: 146). King Abdullah's involvement in the war changed Jordan dramatically and thus led to the incorporation of a large part of Palestine, including Jerusalem, and a fundamental change in Jordan's demographic situation with the Palestinians making up more than half of the population.

Israel: The New State
The State of Israel was the fulfilment of the Zionist dream. The first tasks were to establish the political organizations, such as a government and an army but there were numerous other tasks. First, there were various methods of integration and absorption for the new groups of immigrants. The two major groups were the Sephardic and the Ashkenazy Jews which were able to co-exist but differed dramatically with their respectively African and European/Russian cultural background and education. The tools used to create citizenship were for example the unions, the Histandrut (workers' union), political institutions, the army and the Hebrew language (Yapp 1996: 281). In spite of the efforts to create a citizenry, it is today often argued that a nation was never created, which appears to be a problem haunting Israel over 50 years later. Secondly, Israel's economy witnessed a GNP growth rate at nearly 10% per year but with an annual investment of 25% of the national income. The resources came from the Diaspora, German repatriations and later US aid. Also, a well-educated population, the inflow of cheap labour and the ability to use the Palestinian work force benefited the new state. Thirdly, Israel quickly developed a sophisticated technology industry, which focused on areas such as diamond cutting and weapons production.

The Suez Crisis
Gamal Abdul Nasser came to power in 1954 following the Egyptian revolution in 1952. Egypt's relations to the new Jewish state were tense

and during 1955 relations deteriorated even further, among other things, with the Egyptian blockade of the Strait of Tiran (Yapp 1996: 404). Contrary to the Israeli Defense Forces (IDF), the Egyptian army had not excelled in battle, a fact of which Nasser was very aware. The army was lacking modern weaponry, and in September 1955 Nasser made a deal with the USSR to buy arms via Czechoslovakia. With the Cold War and containment high on the Western political agenda, the move caused a furore because it was assumed that Egypt had joined the Soviet camp. In December 1955, the USA agreed to finance parts of the projected Aswan Dam but less than a year later in July 1956, after Nasser's overtures to Communist China, the offer was withdrawn and Nasser responded swiftly by nationalizing the Suez Canal Company on 26 July 1956 (Yapp 1997: 407).

This did not go down well in Europe. The Protocol of Sèvres was negotiated in France from 22–24 October 1956. It described how Israel, Great Britain and France planned to attack Egypt with the aim of overthrowing Nasser.

> Israel would be invited to attack the Egyptian army in Sinai and pose a
> threat to the Suez Canal and this would provide Britain and France with
> the pretext to activate their military plans and occupy the Suez Canal
> Zone, ostensibly in order to separate the combatants and protect the canal
> (Shlaim 1997: 511).

The plan was orchestrated by France, supported by Israel and reluctantly agreed to by Britain, all having their different motivations. France was still heavily involved in Algeria and furious over Nasser's Arab nationalist rhetoric and support of the Algerian rebels, and some naively believed that removing Nasser would lead to the collapse of the Algerian rebellion (Shlaim 1997: 514). Britain was prepared to fight Nasser over the control of the Suez, yet Prime Minister Eden was nervous about Britain's standing in the Arab world should it venture into an alliance with Israel against an Arab country. Both France and Britain were willing to seek a diplomatic solution, but the military preparations were made, should the negotiations come to naught (Shlaim 1997: 511).

Another dimension of the Sèvres meeting, which took place after the formal negotiations, was the French and Israeli discussions on nuclear technology. In September 1956, France had agreed to supply Israel with the necessary material and know-how to build a smaller, civilian nuclear reactor. At Sèvres the deal was confirmed and after Suez, in

September 1957, France actually supplied a nuclear reactor twice the capacity originally promised (Shlaim 1997: 523). Shlaim argues that since the nuclear dimension was only brought up after the war collusion had been formally agreed, it showed that 'the French were determined to go to war at almost any price and for their own reasons', not because of Israel. Rather, it showed which price France was willing to pay to get Israel to participate in the *'menage a trois'* against Egypt (Shlaim 1997: 524). From Israel's perspective, the Egyptian weapons deal and the closure of the Straits of Tiran presented two good reasons to intervene in Egypt and in addition to this Israel was interested in destroying Nasser's air force (Shlaim 1997: 517). Furthermore, a successful battle might have forced Nasser to recognize Israel and end the so-called state of 'no-war, no-peace' and Sèvres showed that Israel's main interest was the possibility of a military partnership with France (Shlaim 1997: 524).

On 29 October 1956, Israel invaded Sinai which quickly set off Egyptian counter-attacks. As Israel and Egypt refused to cede to the British and French ultimatum, France and Britain bombarded the Egyptian positions. The financial costs of the operation soon increased dramatically and threatened the British economy and Britain was forced either to request financial assistance from the US, or withdraw entirely from the fighting. Britain turned to the US who refused to grant any form of assistance and even condemned the attacks. For France and Britain the war was over. For Nasser the Suez was a triumph and made him the undisputed but still informal leader of the Arab world.

The Suez Crisis marked a turning point on several different levels. First, during the mandatory periods and occupations, the Arab world had been more or less isolated from international relations because the European powers, Britain in particular, had 'naturally' managed the foreign relations. After Suez, the Middle East became a battleground for Cold War rivalry between the US and the USSR with the region becoming, unfortunately perhaps, a much more visible part of international politics. Secondly, for Britain and France, Suez was a disaster. They lost their influence and the secured access to raw materials and lines of communication. In sum, with the Suez crisis, Europe ceased to exist as a dominant power in the Middle East, politically as well as economically.

3 |

Europe and the Middle East from 1956 to 1969

The International System and the Cold War

The explanation and understanding of the Cold War, its origins and development and eventual conclusion has been, and still is, the subject of intense debate among scholars. The purpose of this section is, thus, merely to outline the most central themes and issues that came to influence Europe and the Middle East—and their relations—between 1956 and 1969.

The origins of the Cold War were to be found in Europe. Some argue that a defining moment in the Cold War was the Truman Doctrine in 1947 whereby the USA announced that it would assist states which perceived themselves as threatened by subversion or expansionist moves by the Soviet Union. The Truman Doctrine was formulated in response to the instability in Europe—that is, Greece and Turkey—where, as it was argued, there was a fear of a Communist takeover. The Truman Doctrine was later substantiated with the policy of Containment and the Marshall Plan, which provided a boost to the development of postwar Europe, but also served to draw the line between East and West. This happened as the Eastern European states, pressured by Moscow, were forced to decline the US offer of financial assistance. During the late 1940s and early 1950s, Eastern European governments were being replaced by Marxist-Leninist regimes controlled by, or at least loyal to the USSR. In other words, the division of Europe with the creation of the two blocs had become a reality (Scott 1997: 76-77).

The Berlin crisis of 1948 was perceived by some as the first major Cold War confrontation, which among other things led to a large US military deployment to Europe. In the light of this, the North Atlantic Treaty Organization (NATO) was established in 1949 with the main purpose of committing the US to the defence of Western Europe. The central concept of NATO was that an 'attack on one member would be treated as an attack on all' (Scott 1997: 77). With a US commitment to the defence of Europe yet another dimension was added to the Cold War scenario, namely a military build-up in Europe, not only of conventional weapons but also of nuclear weapons.

The death of Stalin in 1953 improved the international political climate slightly. In the USSR the new leader, Nikita Khruschev, introduced some degrees of modernization, which spilled over into Eastern Europe and led, among other things, to the Soviet invasions of Hungary and Czechoslovakia in the mid-1950s. Some argue that the Franco-British excursion to the Suez in 1956, dealt with in the previous chapter, moderated the international response to the Soviet invasions. The early 1960s, notably with the Berlin Crisis in 1961 and the Cuba Crisis in 1962, marked the period where the risk of a military and perhaps even nuclear confrontation was regarded as very high. During the mid-1960s the superpower relations stabilized somewhat, although the nuclear arms race remained (Scott 1997: 78).

The Middle East after 1956

A decade of post-World War II Arab politics can be approached from many different perspectives. A 'dimensional approach' to the region would suggest not only an approach to the historical development, but also draws attention to the multiplicity and the nuances of the issues facing the Middle East. First, the 'domestic dimension' calls for an understanding of the internal situation of a country where the cornerstone remains the issue of transition from traditional to modern society as well as from colonial status to independence (see Chapter 2). Secondly, the 'regional dimension' (excluding the Arab–Israeli conflict) is the inter-state relations of the Arab world which have been dominated, among other things, by the hegemonic ambitions of different states in the region, usually under the ideological mantle of pan-Arabism. Thirdly, an 'Arab–Israeli dimension', some would argue, should concern itself merely with the bilateral and/or multilateral relations between Israel and the Arab states. The Palestinian–Israeli relations would demand a 'dimension' of its own. Though this is true, at least for now, both aspects will be included in the 'Arab–Israeli dimension' for convenience. Fourthly, during the Cold War, the 'Great Power dimension' evolved primarily around the US–USSR relationship and their jockeying for position and influence in the region. It is important to emphasize that each dimension has a dynamic of its own and is frequently affected by events in the other dimensions (Safran 1992: 357-58).

The Regional Dimension
The most important regional events in the Middle East during the 1950s and 1960s often evolved around, or can be explained by the notion of pan-Arabism. Egypt's President Nasser was the leader of the pan-Arabism, and he sought to create 'one Arab nation' with Egypt as the nucleus. The Ba'ath party which dominated in Syria at that time, and later in Iraq, was also strongly supportive of the notion of Arab unity. The unification of Egypt and Syria between 1958 and 1961 as the United Arab Republic (UAR) was a result of this search for Arab unity. In spite of the failure of the UAR, several Arab integration attempts were launched during the following decade, but all came to naught. As a countermove to the UAR, Jordan and Iraq sought by federation to strengthen the relations between the two Hashemite monarchies and establish an alternative centre of power in Baghdad.

In Lebanon, the delicate balance between the Christians and Muslims broke down as a result of disagreement between President Chamoun who was trying to ensure Lebanon's credentials as a pro-Western country and the Muslim and pan-Arabist opposition, which was supported by the Syrians (the UAR). As a result of the tensions the country descended into civil war. Iraq had always been strongly opposed to Nasser, and the Iraqi leadership decided to provide military assistance to President Chamoun. However, instead of going against Syria, Iraqi troops performed a *coup d'état* in 1958 when the Prime Minister and the royal family were murdered, and Iraq was subsequently proclaimed a republic. Inter-regional conflict was soon complemented by great power dimension. After the Iraqi coup, the Lebanese President requested military assistance from the US, which arrived promptly. The US had been deeply concerned about the loss of the allied Iraq and feared that Lebanon would also succumb to anti-Western political influence. The US action was justified in the Cold War context whereby the US, according to the so-called Eisenhower Doctrine, promised to extend assistance to any country which might be threatened by Communist takeover. Simultaneously, Britain, under the Anglo-Jordanian Treaty, despatched troops to strengthen Jordan's position. In sum, at a stroke Iraq had changed from being Egypt's strongest Arab enemy to a more pro-Arab nationalist republic. In Lebanon, a moderate government was formed and also there the policy changed to a more pro-Arab line (Mansfield 1992: 263). The failure of Arab unity destabilized regional relations further. Following the death of the Imam of Yemen, Egypt ventured into Yemen in 1962 in support of the republican forces. Saudi Arabia supported the Conservatives in Yemen, who still believed in the authority of the Imamate. As a result, Yemen descended into a civil war between the two sides, which lasted until 1967.

The Arab–Israeli Dimension
During the 1960s two non-state actors emerged on the political scene in the Middle East. One was the Arab League and the other was the Palestine Liberation Organization (the PLO). The League of Arab States (the Arab League) was actually created in Cairo on 22 March 1945. Its aim was to ensure and maintain cooperation between the member states, and function as an arbitrator should a conflict between member states arise (Jawad 1992: 4). To seek a resolution by negotiation via the Arab League has later been broadly referred to as an 'Arab solution'.

In 1964 the Arab League established the PLO. Before 1964 most aspects of Palestinian politics had been incorporated into the ideological framework of pan-Arabism. Between 1964 and 1967 the PLO was rendered largely inefficient due to internal disagreements and strong opposition from Palestinian movements, like the Fatah and the Arab Nationalist Movement, because of the Egyptian president Gamal Abdel Nasser's control of the organization. It was to take more than two decades before the PLO was to achieve international recognition and one of the main reasons was the wording of the PLO National Charter. One of the features of the Charter, which was endorsed at the founding conference in 1964, was the assertion that it 'proposed the establishment of a united Palestinian State with the same boundaries as mandatory Palestine' (Yapp 1997: 303). The way to achieve the liberation of Palestine was, at least according to the 1968 amendment of the Charter, by armed struggle, that is, the destruction of the State of Israel.

King Hussein of Jordan was not pleased with the new organization. Jordan and the Palestinian issue are interrelated because the remaining parts of Palestine, that is the West Bank, Jerusalem and the Palestinian refugees who settled in Jordan, were under Jordan's control. King

Hussein promoted himself as the representative of the Palestinians and this explained King Hussein's intense interest and Jordanian sensitivity towards all aspects of the issue. In relation to Jordan, Nasser supported guerrilla attacks on Israel from Jordanian soil and Syria supported among others, al-Fatah. The attacks launched from Jordan were undermining the king's authority and the Israeli military reprisals were always aimed at Jordan, which King Hussein could not accept in the long run.

In 1964 Israel diverted water resources from the River Jordan which, in short, became the first step towards the June War in 1967. The move was perceived as a serious threat and led to the establishment of a joint military command led by Nasser who also began efforts to improve inter-Arab relations. In February 1966, yet another coup took place in Syria where a radical wing of the Ba'ath party came to power. The Ba'ath party intensified the actions against Israel and beefed up its support of al-Fatah. During the spring of 1967, al-Fatah increased its attacks against Israel and, moreover, Israel and Syria clashed with greater frequency on the Golan Heights. On 14 May Egyptian political manoeuvres led to the withdrawal of the UN Emergency Forces from Sinai that had functioned as a buffer between Egypt and Israel, and thus opened the possibility for an Egyptian attack on Israel. The following day, Egypt took Sharm el-Shayk and Nasser closed the Straits of Tiran, which was considered by Israel as justification to take up arms. As a consequence of the Syrian–Egyptian military relations and the increased level of tensions, reluctantly, Jordan joined the existing Egyptian–Syrian military defence pact on 30 May.

On 5 June 1967 Israel attacked Egyptian positions in a pre-emptive strike. In six days Israel captured the Sinai, the West Bank, Gaza and the Golan Heights. The war was a disaster for the Arab world, but clearly a triumph for Israel. Nasser's reputation was seriously damaged and Egypt suffered great losses of both personnel and infrastructure. The war became a catastrophe for Jordan with the loss of the West Bank and a new wave of immigrants. Many naturalized Jordanians (Palestinians from the 1948–49 wave of immigrants) and new immigrants blamed the monarchy for the loss of the West Bank and Jerusalem. During the next decade the increasing support and demands of the PLO soon became highly problematic for the Hashemite monarchy. Its credibility as the future liberator of Palestine as well as its claim to be the representative of the Palestinians living on the West Bank and in

Jordan proper had been seriously imperilled. These events also created mistrust between King Hussein and Yasser Arafat, which was to hamper future attempts of establishing an efficient dialogue between the two parties (Mansfield 1992: 420). The war of 1967 confirmed Israel's military superiority over any combination of Arab forces. In the immediate aftermath of the war the Arab world, especially Jordan, attempted to pursue a policy of accommodation and aimed for a state of non-belligerency. The rationale was the Israeli Defense Forces was perceived to be stronger, and for the moment the Arabs had no wish to tempt fate. Additionally, the PLO performed far below expectation, which led to changes within the organization when several political and military resistance groups joined the PLO and in 1969, Yasser Arafat of the Fatah was elected Chairman of the PLO Executive Committee, a post he holds to this day (Jensen and Laursen 2000: 16).

The Great Power Dimension
The interest of the US and the USSR vis-à-vis the Middle East was to gain influence in the region because of its strategic position and its natural resources. The Middle Eastern states utilized the attention of the superpowers to pursue not regional, but primarily national military and politico-economic interests, which consequently strengthened the focus on the new nation states. For example, the sale of arms to the region imposed heavy economic burdens on the governments, but it enabled them to pursue conflicts at a higher level of aggression and it increased their ability to act independently of the patron superpower. Nevertheless, it was still only the superpowers that could muster sufficient power to influence the final outcome of national or regional conflicts by using the threat of intervention and/or withdrawal of logistical support. As the Cold War intensified, the superpowers sought to maintain a political and military status quo. In other words, there was a security overlay which meant that the superpowers were incapable of preventing war, but they would secure the survival of its client state/ally. The US would thus never let Israel be defeated, and it seemed highly unlikely that the USSR would accept a Syrian defeat. In spite of this, with the Middle East being merely a component of the global superpower rivalry, there was an absence of interest in addressing the root causes of the regional and national concerns and conflicts that haunted the region (Roberson 1998: 5-6). This had also become evident in the post-1967 peace negotiations.

Peace negotiations and the United Nations Security Council Resolution 242

The United Nations Security Council Resolution (UNSCR) 242 condemned the acquisition of territories by force and called for the

> i) Withdrawal of Israel armed forces from territories occupied in the recent conflict, ii) Termination of all claims or states of belligerency and respect for and acknowledgement of the sovereignty, territorial integrity and political independence of every State in the area and their right to live in peace within secure and recognized boundaries free from threats or acts of force (UNSCR 242 in POLI–115EN 1999: 115).

The UNSCR 242 was the result of an unusual alliance of the US, the Soviet Union, France and Britain, the latter being the driving force behind the resolution. The USA and the Soviet Union had been in favour of the resolution because of fear of being entangled in a regional conflict between client proxies, which ultimately could lead to a superpower confrontation. The Soviet Union gained increased influence in the Arab world via its support of UNSCR 242 and its alliance with Egypt. However, the emergence of a stronger PLO hostile to the Soviet allies/client states in the region and, on the other hand, Israel supported by the USA made it important for the Soviet Union to avoid escalation of conflicts in the region, and instead search for a peace settlement. Therefore, it could be argued that the Soviet Union became a '*status quo power*' in the Middle East (Calvocoressi 1982: 226).

The problem with UNSCR 242 was that the resolution was deliberately vaguely formulated and thus open to interpretations, so progress in negotiations based on 242 was consequently hard to achieve. Moreover, there was no direct mentioning of the Palestinians as a people, which was one of the reasons it was rejected by most Arabs. They could *in principle* accept a free, democratic and multi-religious Palestine, but as this clearly was not to emerge they intensified their attacks on Israel instead. Still, it could also be argued that UNSCR 242 reflected an attempt to accommodate both Israel and the Arab states— and the absence of any mention of the Palestinian people can be explained by the state-centred structure of the UN. As said, the Cold War may have been one of the reasons why there was no serious attempt to address the causes of the conflict, but instead maintain a status quo. Alternatively, one may wonder what lay behind Israel's attitude to a peace agreement. Israel had clearly been confirmed as a military hegemon in the region, but as it appeared she adopted a 'wait and see attitude' and the actual desire for a comprehensive peace deal appeared questionable.

Summing up, in the aftermath of the war there were now at least five issues that had become a part of the agenda whenever the discourse fell on the peace negotiations in the Arab–Israeli conflict and the need for a comprehensive peace agreement:

- the question of the status/control over Jerusalem;
- the fate of the Palestinian refugees outside of Israel, the West Bank and Gaza;
- the right of the Palestinian refugees to return to Israel;
- the future of the Golan Heights;
- the future of the West Bank and Gaza (from 1967 also referred to as the Occupied Territories).

After this overview of the historical development, the next step will be to turn to Europe and identify the national interests of the founding members of the European Community vis-à-vis the Middle East. This is important in order to improve our understanding of their behaviour as members of the Community when it comes to formulating Community policies and interests in the Middle East.

The Six Europeans and the Middle East

The purpose of this section is to provide an overview of the relations between the first six European EEC member states (France, the Federal Republic of Germany, the Netherlands, Belgium, Italy and Luxembourg) and the Middle East. Because of its small size, Luxembourg will not receive any mention.

France

After Suez, France under the Fourth Republic (pre-1958) chose to focus on relations to Algeria and exhibit strong support for the nascent Jewish state. However, under the Fifth Republic, De Gaulle initiated a strategic change in France's foreign policies. First, he sought to establish a global policy profile for France, independent of that of the USA and the USSR. This also included the search for an internationally supported/global solution to the Middle East crisis. Secondly, France sought to improve relations with the Arab World without damaging relations with Israel more than necessary (Ifestos 1987: 418-19).

France's relation to the Arab world was complicated. With the memory of Suez still lingering, it was only after Algeria gained her independence in 1962 and the French opposition to Nasser was softened that France was able to conduct a more balanced policy towards the Arab-Muslim world. It was also only then that France was able to assume the role as mediator between the Community and the Maghreb.

The interests that drove the French involvement were the need for a supply of raw materials, especially oil, from the region and, eventually, the export of arms to the region. Already, then, France preferred a system of bilateral relations and the freedom to conduct national initiatives, which inevitably hampered Community efforts. France was prevented from furthering the plans for a coherent Mediterranean Community approach because of domestic opposition, especially from the agricultural sector, which feared the competition from the North African countries.

France's relations to the Middle East especially during the June 1967 war should also be seen in an international context, especially in relation to the Atlantic Alliance. In 1967, France declared that each state in the region had a right to live, and that France would refuse to support any state that took up arms against another. This meant that France refused to grant military support to the countries involved in the 1967 war, including Israel. This shocked the latter profoundly and laid the basis for the following mistrust and scepticism of European involvement in the Middle East and the Middle East peace process. One of the reasons behind this loosening of ties with Israel was that France regarded the US–Israeli link to be primarily of strategic interest for the US (Imperiali and Agate 1984: 1-4).

The French u-turn was to have significant implications for the future relationship between Israel and France, and as a consequence also the long-term relations to the European Union. Israel had regarded France as a key ally until France left Israel alone in the cold in an extremely serious crisis. As a consequence Israel lost complete faith in France— and Europe—and turned to the only alternative ally, the USA.

The Federal Republic of Germany

The Federal Republic of Germany (West Germany) did not formulate a clear Middle East policy until the late 1960s (Steinbach 1984: 91). In the immediate postwar era West Germany was primarily focused on domestic issues, and with events during World War II in Germany vis-à-vis the Jews, the Middle East was deemed a far too sensitive area in which to be engaged politically until the emergence of the European Community's joint approach. Nevertheless, Arabs expected West Germany to lend support to their problems regarding security and political issues. With World War II in mind there was a clear demand from Israel that German policies towards the region should reflect the special obligations that the Germans felt towards the Jews (Steinbach 1984: 93). This attitude held sway for some time, but as the generations changed the nature of the collective memories and guilt complexes of the people, the attitude towards Israel began to change during the 1970s. Having said this, the Middle East remained a sensitive issue in German politics.

From the 1950s, West Germany paid some $1 billion in repatriations to the Holocaust victims living in Israel. The inflow of external capital contributed significantly to the economic development of the new state (Ismael 1986: 98). Moreover, Germany's interest in the Arab–Israeli conflict was to support efforts to reach a settlement, which would secure the state of Israel and make room for a peaceful co-existence between Arabs and Israelis. As Germany began to export arms to the Arab world as well as to Israel, it added to the need for the German government to walk a fine line with regard to formulating its policies towards the Middle East (Steinbach 1984: 93). Diplomatic relations with Israel were established in 1965.

The Netherlands
For centuries the foreign policy of the Netherlands has been guided by three major objectives: 'promoting and protecting its foreign trade, maintaining its national security, and promoting international legal order' (Soedentorp 1984: 37). After the war the Netherlands, which had been occupied by Germany, perceived the Atlantic Alliance as the key to its own security as a small European state and thus supported it wholeheartedly. In relation to the Arab–Israeli conflict, the Netherlands has often been perceived as being strongly in favour of Israel, mainly because of the guilt connected to the extermination of 70% of the Dutch Jewry during the war (Soedentorp 1984: 38). A closer examination will reveal that even though there are elements of truth in the statement, Dutch Middle East policies are just as much bound in the aforementioned interests.

During the late 1940s and early 1950s, the crucial interest for the Netherlands was to retain the Dutch East Indies, or at least ensure that economic links would be maintained should absolute control become impossible. With the Muslim population in Indonesia and in the Arab World the Dutch government had no interests in antagonizing anyone over the question of the partition of Palestine and the subsequent question of the recognition of Israel. Therefore, the Dutch participation on the UN committee on Palestine was justified with reference to the Dutch support of the UN and international law. When the Netherlands supported the British–French initiative in the Suez, it was interpreted as an attempt to force Nasser to comply with international law. Since 1956, the Dutch supported the Israeli demand for a guarantee of free passage of Israeli shipping though the Straits of Tiran as an international waterway. The policy was restated when Nasser closed the Straits on the eve of the June War, again with a reference to the upholding of international law. After the June War, the Netherlands was of the view that territories occupied by Israel should not be annexed unilaterally and any peace accord should be reached within the context of UNSCR 242. The Netherlands granted full recognition to Israel in 1950 (Soedentorp 1984: 38-40).

Belgium

The role of Belgium has been that of a conciliator and moderator in the Arab–Israeli conflict, especially in relation to the superpowers during the Cold War, and thus an advocate of negotiations—a typical small state strategy (Dosenrode 1993: 95). With regard to the Arab–Israeli conflict, there are two events which became turning points for Belgium's policies towards the region. The first was the creation of the state of Israel and its admission to the UN, and the second was the June War. Belgium's policies favoured the new Israeli state up until the June War in 1967. During the Suez crisis Belgium, like the Netherlands, argued in favour of upholding international law and criticized Nasser for his blockade. Belgium demanded that the international waterways were to be respected, and it emphasized the authority of the UN and a need for a solution under the auspices of the UN. The major concern for Belgium was to repair the split in the Atlantic Alliance over Suez. Moreover, Belgium also saw it in her interest not to have France alienated because of Belgian interest in furthering the European integration project as well as because of Belgium's foreign policy tradition. After the June War, UNSCR 242 covered Belgium's interests: recognition of the national sovereignty of every state in the region and recognition of international borders, guaranteed freedom to navigate in international waterways and the denouncing of all acts of violence in the area. Subsequently, and this was to mark a turning point, Belgium would condemn all acts of violence committed by both Arabs and Israelis and thus achieve a more even-handed approach to the region in its later policies (Raeymaeker 1984: 65-66).

Italy

Italy lost her colonial possessions in Africa after World War II. After UN mediation Libya was also relinquished in 1956. Oil was discovered there in 1959. With Italy's decolonialization of the Middle East, as with other European states, the nature of relations with the region changed towards diplomatic relations, ideally built on 'a more co-operative basis', focusing on economic issues and culture (Ismael 1986: 98-99). Although Italy sought to establish diplomatic relations and improve trade relations between the two countries, the Libyan Revolution of 1969 and the coming to power of Colonel Ghadaffi were to complicate relations. In 1970 he confiscated Italian possessions in the country and expelled all Italians. Still, Italy's position vis-à-vis Europe and the Middle East was not uncomplicated. Italy had a strong interest in good relations with the Mediterranean countries but economically it was not strong enough to withstand the challenges of competition. If a coherent Mediterranean policy could be agreed upon, then Italy's position would change from a country situated on the periphery of the EEC, to a country placed centrally in a much larger integrated framework. From a security point of view, Italy had a stronger interest in the creation of a Mediterranean policy than had the Nordic states in Europe.

EC Cooperation with the Middle East

From a European perspective, during the 1960s the main concern for the member states of the EC was to further the process of integration and to establish internal trade and agricultural policies. As described above, the founding six members of the EC conducted their own bilateral trade relations, but 'the economic relations between the European Community and the Arab world before 1972 can be characterized as random, unsystematic and on a case-by-case basis' (Jawad 1992: 7).

It was Italy who in 1964 expressed a desire for a so-called global co-operation between the EC and the Mediterranean countries, which was to include the establishment of a free trade area, the distribution of aid and some concessions for the Mediterranean agricultural sector. However, at first the proposal did not receive a favourable response in the Council. In 1966, the Commission made an unsuccessful proposal for a 'global' policy towards the Maghreb. A result of this stalemate was that the Commission went it alone and utilized perhaps the only foreign policy tool at its disposal, namely the establishment of trade co-operation agreements (Jawad 1992: 21). Therefore, during the 1960s the only deals concluded were the preferential trade agreements with the North African countries of Morocco, Tunisia and Algeria, which were concluded in 1969. Regarding the Middle East, Lebanon (1965) and Egypt (1972) were the only countries with a similar agreement with the EC (Jawad 1992: 7).

The EC's deal with Lebanon was a non-preferential trade agreement, which was signed in May 1965 and came into force in July 1968. The agreement included both trade—mutual granting of the 'most favoured nation treatment'—and technical cooperation where the EC would conduct surveys of Lebanese resources, set up research institutions, and provide technical training and equipment to Lebanon. However, trade relations developed in favour of the EC and the technical cooperation never got off the ground. Therefore, Lebanon requested a re-negotiation of the agreement, which resulted in a preferential agreement being signed in 1972 (Jawad 1992: 18-19).

Egypt's preferential trade agreement came into force in December 1973 and aimed towards the establishment of a free trade area (Jawad 1992: 20). With regard to the former North African countries, it was France who insisted on maintaining economic relations to colonies and other overseas territories under her (partial) control. This resulted in a protocol annexed to the Treaty of Rome, which granted Morocco and Tunisia a privileged access to the French markets (Jawad 1992: 10-11).

The Algerian case was different. At the time of the signing of the Treaty of Rome Algeria was considered a part of France and treated accordingly, that is, that the Treaty of Rome would include Algeria as a part of France. After its independence in 1962, the EC continued its preferential trade agreements with the country. Nevertheless, soon after independence Algeria sought to renegotiate the agreement, but this was refused by the Community—primarily because of the delicate political relations between Algeria and the neighbouring countries on the one hand, and the Community on the other.

During the late 1960s, the EC began to feel a growing sense of frustration with the differing ways of applying the preferential trade system used by the Community members towards North Africa. The problem with Algeria especially, led to a gradual realization that there was a need for a revision and reorganization of relations. Still, member states such as West Germany and the Netherlands were not in favour of establishing a Mediterranean policy as this would be a clear signal of the EC venturing into a new internationalist role. This could complicate relations with the USA, which was opposed to a Community approach to the Mediterranean, and their preference was still to ensure the Atlantic Alliance. However, the position of the two states, as well as that of the new members, Denmark and the UK, changed during the early 1970s which eventually paved the way for the 'Mediterranean Policy' which was launched in 1972.

A Common Foreign Policy Approach in the Making? Foreplay to the Hague Summit of 1969
If economic relations with the Middle East and the North African countries were somewhat disorganized, then the foreign policy coordination of the EC was non-existent. The June War of 1967 demonstrated with unpleasant clarity the impotence of the EC with regards to foreign policy coordination. At the Rome summit which took place shortly before the war broke out, the national interests of the member states were too different to reconcile. German Chancellor Kiesinger declared: 'I felt ashamed at the Rome Summit. Just as the war was on the point of breaking, we could not even agree to talk about it' (Ifestos 1987: 420). Shortly afterwards, the national policies were shown through the reaction of the member states to the war: France condemned Israel and supported the Arabs in the UN debates. Italy also supported the Arab side. Officially, Germany emphasized its neutrality but remained strongly supportive of Israel. The Netherlands adopted a pro-Israeli stand, and Belgium put its faith in the international organizations like the UN and the Atlantic Alliance (Ifestos 1987: 420). After the end of the war in 1967 and up until 1969 there was no coordination of EC policies towards the Arab–Israeli conflict. With the War of Attrition that followed the 1967 June War, France attempted to influence the shaping of events in the region. In order to reach a settlement, France sought in vain to establish a 'four power meeting' with the USA, the USSR and the UK.

The sense of failure as well as the increased potential of creating a role for the EC in international relations encouraged the Community to seek alternative ways of creating a global role for itself. With the departure of de Gaulle from the French presidency a major internal stumbling block disappeared. The introduction of the plan for the European Political Cooperation took place at the Hague Summit in 1969 and marked a 'breaking point' for the Community in its role as an international actor in the making.

4 |

The European Community and the Middle East from 1969 to 1991

This chapter will analyse the period of Middle East policy which, for many, is considered archetypical for the troubled region as well as for the EC's attempts to act in international politics. During this time, one crisis in the Middle East rapidly followed the other, with numerous hopes for peace, and with interventions by the superpowers. The chapter will begin by taking a short look at the developments in the international system, and then proceed to give an overview of what happened in the Middle East up to 1989 and then from 1989 to 1991 before analysing the European Community's approach to the Middle East.

Developments in the International System 1969–1989

The period began with détente between the USA and USSR, developed into the New Cold War (1979–85), and ended with Perestroika, the collapse of the Soviet Union and the emergence of the 'New International World Order' (1989). From a security political viewpoint the period ranged from close to real peace to verging on nuclear war, and then to peace.

The period began in the middle of the détente. After the 1962 Cuban missile crisis brought the world close to nuclear disaster, the two superpowers slowly began rethinking their relations. 'Détente had its roots in mutual recognition of the need to avoid nuclear crisis, and in the economic and military incentives in avoiding an unconstrained arms race' (Scott 1997: 78). In Europe, German Chancellor Willy Brandt's 'Ostpolitik' had helped to pave a road for détente. To reach the goal of détente, the US strategy was:

> Predicated on the expectation that the development of economic, political, and strategic ties between the United States and the Soviet Union would bind the two in a common fate, linkage would make

superpower relations dependent on the continuation of mutually reward-
ing exchanges. In this way, linkage would lessen the superpowers'
incentives for war (Kegley and Wittkopf 1995: 65).

Visible signs of détente were the Strategic Arms Limitation Talks
(SALT) I and II. The first was signed in 1972, and entered into force.
The latter was signed in 1979, but was not ratified due to suspicion by
the US Congress towards the USSR; their suspicion was seen by many
as justified when the Soviet Union invaded Afghanistan in 1979 and
finally ending the epoch of détente. During this period the European
states enjoyed a certain freedom of action, which then elapsed.

The period from 1979 to 1985 has been labelled the 'New Cold War'
or the 'Second Cold War'. Beginning under US President Carter it was
carried on by President Reagan (US president 1988), who referred to
the USSR as 'the Evil Empire'. These were the last years of the orthodox
Communists in power in the USSR (Brezhnev, Andropov, Chernenko).

> The legitimating myth of the Soviet Union, Marxism-Leninism, was
> antithetical to that of the United States, Lockean liberalism. The United
> States and the Soviet Union were rivals not only because they were the
> poles in a bipolar world, but also because their governing ideologies
> were so fundamentally at odds (Krasner 1997: 201).

Two initiatives are symbolic for this period. The first was the 'Dual
Track Decision' of NATO to deploy 108 Pershing II missiles and 464
Cruise missiles in Europe by 1983, unless arms reduction talks with the
Soviet Union made this step superfluous. The NATO decision was
considered a counterweight to the superior Soviet conventional forces,
as well as countering the increased Soviet deployment of SS 20
missiles in Eastern Europe. An equally important reason for the NATO
decision was the European wish to secure a US engagement in Europe
in case of a war (Nørretranders 1984). The second initiative was that of
President Reagan to explore the possibility of creating a space-based
defence against ballistic missiles, popularly called 'Star Wars'. This
initiative cooled relations between Moscow and Washington even further. Should the US come up with such a workable system, the teeth of
the Soviet nuclear forces would be drawn. The atmosphere was extremely tense in Europe, which feared it could become a theatre of war.[1]

---

1.   This feeling of being a victim of the superpowers began already in 1977, as
President Carter decided to start producing Neutron bombs and deploying them in
Europe. The N-Bomb kills human beings and animals, but leaves cities intact
(Dosenrode 1993: 174-75).

The change came with the shift of generations in the Soviet Union. General Secretary Mikhail Gorbachov took power in 1985, and soon after introduced 'glasnost' (openness) and 'perestroika' (restructuring). These concepts were intended to reform a socialist Soviet Union, but resulted, in the long run, in bringing it to the edge of collapse. Gorbachov's foreign policy line was to break with old patterns, and end the Cold War arms-race, which had ruined the Soviet economy. Kegley and Wittkopf state:

> Surprisingly, the Soviets did what they promised. They began to act like an ally instead of an enemy. Building on the momentum created by the Intermediate-range Nuclear Forces (INF) agreement signed in 1987, the Soviet Union agreed to end its aid and support to Cuba, withdrew from Afghanistan and Eastern Europe, and announced unilateral reductions in military spending (1995: 98).

The Development in the Middle East 1969–1989[2]

In the Middle East the 20 years between 1969 and 1989 gave rise to both conflicts and hopes for peace, although the first clearly prevailed. 'It has been claimed, that the conflict between Arabs and Israelis is one of the world's most disruptive conflicts, consisting of a mix of religious and nationalistic sentiments as well as the love for one land' (Martin-Diaz 1999: 1). Although it is possible to argue that the following list of events is arbitrary, it gives an impression of a very turbulent and violent period in the region: beginning with the 1969–70 Egyptian–Israeli 'War of Attrition', followed by the 'October' or 'Yom Kippur War' 1973, the first oil crisis 1973, President Sadat's Jerusalem visit 1977 and the following Camp David process 1978–79, the second oil crisis 1979–80, the Iran–Iraq War 1980–88, the invasion of Lebanon 1982, and the beginning of the first Intifada on the West Bank 1987. To provide an overview, a number of key events are analysed separately, although in reality they are closely interlinked, and create a very complex web.

Israeli–Egyptian Relations: From Hot War to Cold Peace

Following the Six Day War of 1967, where Israel had occupied the

---

2. This section, to a considerable degree, builds on chs. 9–15 in J.P.D. Dunbabin's excellent book *The Post-Imperial Age: The Great Powers and the Wider World* (1994a).

whole of Sinai, an insecure cease-fire was implemented. The basis for solving the conflict should have been Resolution 242 of the UN Security Council from November 1967 (see Chapter 3). But peace did not come to the region; the skirmishes escalated during the following years until President Nasser declared an end to the cease-fire. With Egypt's large population Nasser thought that it would be possible to pursue a war of attrition and win it (Dunbabin 1994a: 313). Once more Egyptian forces failed to rise to the test, and after a little more than a year (in July 1970) Egypt, Jordan and Israel accepted a US initiative for a new cease-fire (Report to the [UN] Secretary General 1973; S/10920, p. 29). The help Nasser had sought and received from the Soviet Union had not been enough to stop the Israeli advances. At the peak of détente, neither the USA nor the USSR were willing to risk a major clash over Egypt (Jawad 1992: 64-65).

President Nasser's successor, Anwar Sadat, looked for an opportunity for revenge. Between 1970 and 1973 Egypt followed a double track strategy. They pressed the Soviet Union for weapons and only succeeded after having expelled all Soviet military 'advisors' in 1972. Egypt also tried to interest the USA in playing an active role in the Middle East, but in vain. The Vietnam War, as well as the Watergate scandal, occupied Washington more than the Middle East. Thus, Sadat resolved that only the military option would regain Sinai and put the Middle East back on the international agenda (interview with Sadat, *Newsweek*, 9 April 1973).

Allied with Syria, Egypt attacked Israeli forces in Sinai on 6 October 1973, the Jewish holiday of Yom Kippur. The surprise was total. After immediate success, the luck of war changed, and Israel began regaining her losses, preparing both to march on to Damascus and to encircle the 3rd Egyptian Army (Jawad 1992: 63-64). The road to Damascus was subsequently blocked by Jordanian and Iraqi units. External pressure came first from the USSR (to save the 3rd Army by military force), then from a UN resolution negotiated by the USA and USSR, which ordered a cease-fire, demilitarized zones and so on.[3] A final cease-fire was reached on 25 October.[4] In spite of the near total military defeat,

3.   Security Council Resolution (UNSCR) 338, from 22 October 1973 basically repeated the contents of resolution 242, mentioned above.
4.   The Yom Kippur, or the October War, came close to involving the two superpowers in the conflict especially after Anwar Sadat asked both superpowers to intervene to make Israel accept the 22 October cease-fire. The USSR reacted

only stopped by external intervention, Sadat managed to use the war to boost Arab pride, and place the Middle East on the international agenda (Dunbabin 1994a: 320-24).

The Suez Canal was reopened in 1975, and Israel and Egypt, developed and kept informal contacts. The real breakthrough came as a spin-off from the joint USA–USSR communiqué of October 1977 calling for a peace conference in Geneva to discuss a solution of the Palestinian problem, and Israeli withdrawal from the occupied territories. Israel got upset and President Carter asked Sadat for help to clear the situation. The help came with Sadat's historic decision to visit Israel and to talk to its parliament, Knesset, in November 1977. In spite of the emotional impact, the direct negotiations between Egypt and Israel following the visit did not bring any concrete results, and Sadat considered resigning, basically bringing the situation 'back to normal'. It was then that President Carter joined the process, inviting the parties to Camp David. The result was the March 1979 peace agreement, *inter alia*, handing back Sinai to Egypt. But the agreement did not include a solution of the 'Palestinian Problem', and the agreement resulted in strong Arab opposition and, in a decade the diplomatic isolation of Egypt from the rest of the Arab world (Dunbabin 1994a: 326-29).

The Arab–Persian Conflict: The Iraq–Iranian War
The region's next war was the Iran–Iraq War 1980–88. The relationship between the Arab Iraq and the Persian Iran had ranged between cold peace and war since the previous century among other things due to border disputes (report from the Danish UN Ambassador to the Danish Foreign Ministry No. 610.K.54, 1969). Iran, presumably weakened by the revolution, was attacked by Iraq in September 1980. Iraq hoped to take over the oil-rich, mainly Arab provinces on the other side of the border, and install a new pro-Iraq government in Teheran. A success would both have been an important step on the way to becoming a regional hegemon, and at the same time, would have prevented the export of Muslim fundamentalism. After a year of good luck, Iraqi fortune changed and Iran forces began driving the invasion back. In

positively to the suggestion, the USA negatively. The 25 October cease-fire first came about after the USSR had sent a letter to President Nixon stating that it would have to consider unilateral steps if the 22 October cease-fire was not respected. The USA conceded. But, as already mentioned neither the USA nor the USSR were willing to risk a major clash over Egypt at the peak of détente (Jawad 1992: 64-65).

spite of the 'New Cold War', the two superpowers kept outside. They first began getting involved as Iranian forces attacked Western oil-tankers in the Gulf in 1987. This led to a Western naval build-up, which in turn helped Iran realize that it could not win the war, and both countries accepted a UN cease-fire in August 1988 (Halliday 1998; Nirumand 1990). For the Arab world, the war had three important aspects: first, it helped Egypt back into the warmth as it supported Iraq, thus showing its Arab solidarity; secondly, it did *not* help destroy Iranian attempts to export an Islamic revolution, as had been hoped by most Arab states which were afraid of Islamic fundamentalism in their countries; and thirdly, it did show that 'Arab unity' was a reality, although a weak one. Apart from Syria, most Arab states supported Iraq politically and economically, against Iran after the war had lasted some years.

The Lebanon: A Victim of Regional Conflicts
If it is right to talk of the Iraq–Iran war as going relatively 'unnoticed' by world opinion, the same cannot be said of the Syrian and later the Israeli invasions of Lebanon. After the Six Days War, Jordan had become a major site for Palestinian refugees, including the PLO, which continued raids on Israel across the border. The PLO raids against Israel as well as the presence of armed forces within Jordan put Jordan's security and stability at risk as well as threatened the internal sovereignty of King Hussein. King Hussein of Jordan managed to overthrow and expel the PLO in 1971 after a series of clashes between the PLO and the Jordanian army.

One of the places the PLO established itself was the Lebanon, where it was one of the reasons for the tragedy of the Lebanese civil war. Lebanon had been an old French protectorate, with a mixed Christian–Muslim population. The Lebanese President Frangieh declared in 1973 that he would not tolerate the increased PLO activities against Israel from Lebanese territory. But the Lebanese army proved to be too weak to stop the PLO.

> This led, after clashes in 1973 between the army and the Palestinians, to the build-up of political and confessional militias. In 1975, when Palestinians got involved in a clash between (Muslim) fishermen and the army, Christians responded by campaigning against their continued armed presence. This soon spread to street battles in the capital (Beirut), attacks on a Palestinian refugee camp (Dunbabin 1994a: 316).

Dunbabin's observation implied that the Christian militias did not mind Palestinian refugees staying in Lebanon, as long as they were unarmed and submitted to the Lebanese state. But the PLO did not want this. The fights escalated along confessional lines, and 1975–76 was a regular civil war (Milton-Edwards 2000: 111-14). Soviet-backed Syria intervened in 1976 and this was legitimized at the Arab Riyadh Summit, by renaming the Syrian intervention force the 'Arab Detente Force'. Basically, Syria's intervention suited well Israel's short term needs of relief from Palestinian attacks, but in the long run, it was not in Israel's interest that Syria established a hegemony over Lebanon. Israel, in particular, would not tolerate Syrian troops at the Lebanese-Israeli border. The situation created a vacuum along the border, which allowed continuous Palestinian raids on Israel. In March 1978 Israel invaded Lebanon to stop these raids. The US demanded immediate withdrawal and the UN established a peacekeeping force. Israel withdrew, but supported a militia leader, who declared an 8-mile broad area across Lebanon 'a free state', thus establishing a buffer (Dunbabin 1994a: 316-17).

As the situation deteriorated further in Lebanon, Israel invaded in June 1982, and stayed until June 1985, at one time occupying Beirut. One result of the invasion was the defeat and evacuation of the PLO and its headquarters to Tunisia (Milton-Edwards 2000: 97). The evacuation was secured by a US-French-Italian peacekeeping force, which withdrew in 1984, due to its constant losses following sniper attacks and bombings. Israel partly withdrew in 1985, but Syria remained and secured its position in the country. Some kind of internal peace was secured by 1990, and in 1991 the Lebanese 'government' concluded a treaty of Syrian–Lebanese 'brotherhood, co-operation and co-ordination' (Dunbabin 1994a: 319). In this way Syria, backed by the USSR, formalized its hegemony over Lebanon. Thus we can see that Lebanon was the victim of both the Arab–Israeli conflict, and the hegemonical desires of a 'brethren Arab state', Syria.

The Palestinian Problem Outside Israel
The Palestinian problem is, at least rhetorically, the core of the Arab–Israeli conflict. Nearly any kind of aggression from the Arab side towards Israel or towards other Arab states, is normally justified by reference to this tragic problem. Osama Bin Laden recently argued after the terrorist act on 11 September 2001 against the Pentagon and the

World Trade Center that the USA would never get peace before the Palestine question was solved.

As previously mentioned, the Arab League at its meeting in 1964 created the Palestine Liberation Organization to give the Palestinians an 'official' recognition and to organize the Palestinian opposition to Israel (Bender 1974: 17). Already before the Six Days War in 1967, more than 1.3 million Palestinian refugees lived outside Israel; the main part (722,687) in Jordan (Report of the Commissioner-General of UNRWA for Palestine Refugees in the Near East, 1 July 1966–30 June 1967). The Palestinian refugees' hopes for returning to their homeland were linked to an international agreement on the matter, and these hopes were buoyed carried by supposed Arab solidarity, which has been strong rhetorically.[5] In reality, the Palestinians have often been victims of 'realpolitik'. One such disappointment was US Foreign Secretary Rogers' initiative in 1970 for a cease-fire and peace talks on the basis of UN Resolution 242 (calling for Arab recognition of Israel, as well as Israeli withdrawal from all occupied territories). This would have run counter to the Palestine hope of returning to a Palestine without Israelis (the Palestine National Charter from June 1968). Another catastrophe, seen with Palestinian eyes, was the expulsion of the PLO from Jordan in 1971 ('Black September'), which was carried out to secure both peace within Jordan, and more peaceful Israeli–Jordan relations (Milton-Edwards 2000: 99). Yet, another disappointment was the Egypt–Israeli Peace from 1977, when the Palestine question was only marginalized. After their departure from Jordan, the PLO mainly operated from Lebanon until they were forced to withdraw to Tunisia in 1984. To counter the development of marginalization among its Arab allies as well as internationally, the PLO began a series of terrorist acts from the beginning of the 1970s such as hijackings of airplanes and the massacre of Israeli athletes at the Olympic Games in Munich 1972 (Milton-Edwards 2000: 101).

To sum up, the Palestinian cause has been met with great rhetorical and often monetary support by Arab states, and the PLO was created by them. Still, pan-Arab solidarity with the Palestinians, has often been weak. To quote Milton-Edwards (2000: 101): 'after 1967 the Palestin-

---

5.   In a letter from Abba Eban to the UN Security Council one of Nasser's more aggressive radio speeches is quoted, May 1956, Security Council, Official Records, May–June 1956, p. 71 Document S/3603.

ians realized they could no longer depend on their Arab brethren for liberation, that their fate now rested firmly in their own hands'.

The First Intifada: The Israeli–Arab Conflict 'at Home'
'For many years...it was not particularly difficult [for Israel] to rule [the West Bank and the Gaza Strip]', Dunbabin states (1994a: 331). First, because the administration was taken care of by Arab civil servants paid by Jordan, and, secondly, the Arab population witnessed a reasonable rise in its standard of living as a 'spin off' of working in Israel. But the 'Palestine question' was not forgotten. Following the Camp-David agreement in 1978–79, Egypt and Israel agreed on giving the West Bank and the Gaza strip some degree of autonomy, but the negotiations got nowhere, and the Israeli invasion of Lebanon in 1982 made Egypt break off the negotiations and withdraw its ambassador.

With the PLO exiled in Tunisia, it seemed as if the relatively quiet situation in the occupied territories could go on forever. Thus, most people were taken by surprise when the Palestinian resistance, the Intifada, broke out in 1987. But according to Milton-Edwards (2000: 101, 102), it should not have been any surprise as 'For decades Palestinians and Israelis sought ways to distinguish themselves from each other...rather than [creating] mutual bonds to promote compromise.' and 'By the mid-1980s there were growing resentments within the Palestinian community against the Israeli occupation authorities'.

The Intifada was a locally directed fight, which quickly escalated and had two consequences: First, it put Israel in a bad light, due to the deaths and casualties among the Palestinians, some of whom were mere children, and related to this, secondly it brought the Palestine problem on to the international agenda *inter alia* due to mass-media coverage of the conflict. Following a year of rioting, in 1988, the king of Jordan relinquished any claims to the sovereignty of the West Bank to the PLO, after the PLO had turned down the king's proposal of Jordanian negotiations with Israel; negotiations which should have been conducted with Jordanian diplomats acceptable to the PLO.

The king's action had three effects; first, it prevented a spillover of the Intifada into Jordan; secondly, it paved the way for a Palestinian state; and thirdly, it undermined the king's role as being responsible for Palestine. The same year the PLO proclaimed an independent Palestine state, and the following year set up an exile government (Dunbabin 1994a: 332).

A high ranking Middle Eastern diplomat[6] once described the easiest way to grasp the very complex situation of the Israeli–Palestinian conflict was to look at both population groups as resistance movements, wanting to liberate the same country, Israel. The Zionists won the fight against the British, and the Arabs lost.

Oil: A Source of Wealth and War
One of several factors making the Middle East so important to the West is its oil-reserves. As seen already, the oil industry used to be controlled by Western countries. A first step towards increased independence of the multinational oil companies was the foundation of the Organization of Petroleum Exporting Countries (OPEC) in 1960, thus creating an organization which 13 years later would have a tremendous political impact. The concrete reason for this step was the decision by the seven biggest oil companies (the 'Seven Sisters') to reduce prices in 1959 and 1960 (Chalabi 1997–98: 128). But OPEC had not then gained enough strength to play an important political role, as one saw when some Arab producers tried to use oil as a weapon against the West during the Six Days War, by cutting supplies for UK and USA; it did not have any political importance at all. When Libya's King Idris was overthrown by Colonel Ghadaffi in 1969 (while the European powers and the USA stood passively by) a new epoch began. Colonel Ghadaffi wanted to take control over oil production in his country. This was fairly easy as Dunbabin (1994a: 348) explains: (1) Libya only had a small population, making it less dependent on oil revenues; (2) the Suez Canal had been closed since 1967, making Libyan oil more accessible and thus more important; and (3) the quality of Libyan oil was high, thus hard to replace. The oil companies turned out not to be loyal towards one another, and one by one gave in to Ghadaffi's demands instead of standing united; besides they got no support from their governments. In that way Ghadaffi showed the other OPEC countries (1) that it was possible to win over the mighty oil companies, and (2) that the Western governments did not want to intervene.

In December 1970, OPEC formulated new higher price targets. The oil companies tried to stand united, taught by the Libyan lesson. But OPEC was able to push through its demands. Following the price demands came demands for participation in oil exploitation. In some

6.   Private conversations with the authors of this book.

cases, like Saudi Arabia, one agreed on an immediate 25% share, raising to 51% over ten years; in other countries the governments simply nationalized parts of the oil industry (e.g. Libya, Iraq). By then, OPEC had learned the important lesson of solidarity, which cannot be said of the oil-consuming countries which tried to muddle through with individual agreements.

When the October War broke out in 1973, OPEC realized the dependence of the West on oil resources and simultaneously that the West was more than reluctant to use force. Thus, on a meeting in Kuwait OPEC decided to cut back oil production with 5% per month until Israel had returned the territories occupied after 1967 (*Guardian*, 15 November 1973). Saudi Arabia made a 10% production cut-back, and imposed an oil embargo on USA and the Netherlands, and nearly on Denmark, due to their pro-Israeli stands. The result was the stalling of economic progress in the West, and the beginning of an economic crisis (Chalabi 1997–98: 130). The second oil shock came in 1979–80 and was basically a misinterpretation of the market situation. Due to the fundamentalist takeover in Iran, the country's oil production ceased for a time, followed by a period of a deliberately low output. Once more, the prices rocketed, but the situation normalized faster than in 1973. Ever since, the prices have been more friendly, seen through consumer eyes (Chalabi 1997–98: 130).

The External Powers
All the major conflicts we have discussed so far have involved external powers, mainly the two superpowers, either directly or indirectly. By supplying or refusing to supply weapon or military advisors, by putting political pressure on the states of the region, or by sending armed forces to the region, they have, on the one hand, tried to limit the conflicts to prevent a spillover to the global system, and, on the other hand, have pursued their own national or global interests in the region.

The superpowers began their rivalry in the region in 1946, when the Soviet Union tried to gain control over the Dardanelles and was more than reluctant to withdraw from the north of Iran (Hubel 1991: 50). But the rivalry was still overshadowed by the presence of Great Britain and France in the region, at that time. None of the superpowers had—or have—a geographical stronghold in the region; the Soviet Union tried hard to gain one in Nasser's Egypt, but in vain.

The superpower's interests in the Middle East can be explained in terms of primary and secondary motives. The primary motive in this period is oil: oil reserves, oil production and the transportation of oil (including the opening or closing of the Suez canal). In spite of the USA's own oil-producing capacity, this country and especially its European allies were strongly dependent on a steady supply of energy. The two oil crises showed this clearly. Barnett, quoted in Ifestos (1987: 375) expressed the importance of oil thus:

> Oil is a strategic commodity; its availability and on what terms is as much a part of collective security and mutual support as is NATO and the US security relationship with Japan. The energy vulnerability of the allies affect the overall strategic balance with the USSR.

Thus, the superpower controlling the Middle East controlled the Western economy. This in itself was a motive for the Soviet Union to pursue an active Middle East policy. Should the Soviet Union be able to control the Arab states, it would be able to control the lifeline of the West, thus the Soviet Union conducted an anti-Israeli and pro-Arab Middle East policy. Several quasi-socialist Arab states embraced the possibility of strong relations to the Soviet Union (e.g., Egypt and Syria) to secure arms in the struggle against Israel.

Apart from securing her own and her allies' economic life-line, oil, the USA had two other main motives: first, trade in general was an important motive for the USA, and secondly, it was important to prevent further Soviet-communist expansion, by containment (in the Truman doctrine). The US situation was complicated by her guarantee to secure Israel's independence (also a primary motive), thus pushing aside many quasi-socialist Arab countries, which potentially might have preferred good relations with the USA rather than with the USSR. Still, the USA was able to keep up reasonable contacts with the more conservative Arab states. Among the secondary motives for the Soviet Union were the ideological interest in extending the Marxist-Leninist ideology as well as securing trade partners. Both motives were external in nature, but also of a great domestic significance.

Hubel stressed the important fact that neither superpowers had a secure and stable sphere of influence in the region, and neither were able to create a permanent presence there (1991: 50). Still, they each cultivated their own allies in the Middle East (Krasner, 1997: 201).

A frequently heard statement was (and is) that peace could never prevail in the Middle East unless at least one external great power was present to guarantee it.[7] Perhaps this is a cultural left-over from the centuries under Ottoman rule, when conflicts were tolerated only to a certain level. Still, the period in question taught the Arab countries the dangers of relying too much on extra-regional powers: Great Britain finally withdrew from the Gulf in the beginning of the 1970s, leaving the responsibility for stability mainly to the Shah's Iran, supported by the USA; support that did not turn out particularly successfully, which in turn gave the image of the USA a severe blow. The two superpowers succeeded in three important matters. First, they prevented an escalation of the regional conflicts in the Middle East to a global conflict. Secondly, they each prevented their clients from being totally defeated in the wars. And thirdly, the superpowers were able to cement and expand their own hegemonies in the region—and of the superpowers, the USA was the most important in the region:

> the USA during the period 1973–78 came to be seen by many as an indispensable part of the peace-making process. Many states in the region came to look upon the USA as either protector, a stabilizing influence or a peacemaker (Allen and Smith 1984: 191).

The Middle East 1969–1989: A Region of Conflicts
This section looks at the most important Middle Eastern conflicts of which Sahliyeh claims: 'the Palestinian-Arab-Israeli conflict is potentially the most lethal and volatile…and the most difficult to resolve' (in Milton-Edwards 2000: 96). To try to get an overview of this very complex pattern, one can group the conflicts in four broad categories:

1. Inter-Arab conflicts are rooted in historic, ideological, religious as well as purely power political factors. Perhaps it is possible to divide the major actors in two groups: the 'moderate states', Saudi Arabia, UAE, Kuwait and the more radical ones, Iraq and Syria. Egypt began the period as 'extreme' with solid links to the Soviet Union, and ended it as 'moderate' with reasonable relations to the West. The core of the major tensions were political, that is, the fight over the hegemony over the whole region (Egypt and Iraq), or parts of it (Syria). The more moderate states looked towards the West for part-

7. Several high ranking Middle Eastern diplomats clearly expressed the same towards the authors in Spring 2000. But it was also stated by the then Israeli Defence Minister, Moshe Dayan, as early as in February 1968 (Danish Foreign Office Archives, 119.K.1.a).

ners (Kuwait, Saudi Arabia, UAE) the less moderate looked towards the Soviet Union (Iraq, Syria, for a time also Egypt). But apart from the major tensions, there were numerous 'smaller' conflict potentials: Syria versus Lebanon (Syria's wish for hegemony), Saudi Arabia versus Jordan (over the Hejaz-Province), Syria versus Iraq (rivalry over the Ba'ath Party), Syria versus Jordan (ideological and power political), Saudi Arabia's concerns over Yemen and so forth.

2.   The Arab–Persian conflict is to be seen in connection with the inter-Arab conflict. As well as historic rivalries between Iraq and Iran, Iraq also needed the oil fields of Iran to be able to fulfil its dreams of being the regional hegemon. Other aspects such as the Shia Muslim Iraqis' fear of a Shi'ite Muslim spill-over against the ideology of the ruling Ba'ath Party is another important, albeit subordinated factor to take into account.

3.   The Iraq–Iran conflict was, again, linked to the inter-Arab fight for hegemony in the Arab world, in the form of Iraq's concrete attempt to get access to Kuwait's oil reserves, as it could not get Iran's, and thus, dominate the Arab world.

4.   The Arab–Israeli conflict including the Lebanon problem, and the Palestinian conflict, had at least two main elements. First, it is an Israeli–Arab (Palestinian) conflict over the exclusive right to live in the same country. Secondly, the conflict has been used by Egypt to try to establish itself as the dominant leader of the Arab world, initially quite successfully.

Behind several of these conflicts are the shadows of the two super-powers. Stephen Krasner is very clear about the consequence of the involvement of the two superpowers (1997: 202):

> The Arab–Israeli conflict could be extended through four wars and over forty years because the Arab States, despite four defeats, could still hope that the Soviet Union would give them greater support, or that the United States would become disillusioned with Israel.

With this in mind, the role of the European Community in the region in this period will be examined.

The European Community and the Middle East 1969–1989

In this section, the slow development of a European attitude towards the Middle East is analysed, starting at a point of strong divergences and moving towards a more united approach. The analysis will be divided into two parts; the first includes the period from 1969 until the Venice Declaration in 1980 when the EC as an entity felt forced to formulate a Middle East approach; and the second part analysing the developments from Venice until 1989.

Although it is obviously impossible to treat a state's foreign policy as several segregated policies, for clarity's sake the EC's Middle East policies will be examined as three policies, bearing in mind that they are interlinked:

- the Peace Process (key actor: EPC/CFSP);
- the Global Mediterranean Policy (key actor: EEC);
- the Euro–Arab dialogue (key actors: EPC/CFSP and EEC); leading to the EEC–Gulf Cooperation Council Agreement (key actor: EEC).

The EPC and the Middle East 1969–1973
The six original EC member states and the UK had quite different approaches to the Middle East in the 1960s. Even the Six Days War of 1967 could not produce a common stand; neither among the EC member states, nor among the 'relevant' great powers, the UK, France, Germany and Italy. Especially France, but also Italy, supported the Arab side, Belgium opted for a UN solution, whereas Germany declared herself 'neutral' but *de facto* supported Israel, together with the Netherlands which strongly defended the Israeli cause (Greilsammer and Weiler 1984: 131-32). During the negotiations following the war, President de Gaulle suggested a four power initiative in the beginning of 1969, but it was turned down by the USA.

The Hague meeting of 1969 created European Political Cooperation (EPC), and one of the first topics on its agenda was the Middle East. Within the framework of EPC, a secret report on the Middle East, the so-called 'Schuman document' was agreed on in 1971. Its status was uncertain; France considered it an official policy, others such as Germany and the Netherlands described it as an informal working paper. The content of the paper was, according to Voorhoeve, six points:

> return of the occupied territories to the Arabs, with only the possibility of small frontier changes; recognition of Israel by Arab States; an extra-territorial status for the Holy Places including Jerusalem; a UN Peace-keeping force in a demilitarized zone made up of Israeli and Arab territory; freedom of navigation through the Strait of Tiran and re-

opening of the Suez Canal; and a solution to the Palestinian question (Voorhoeve 1985: 237).

The paper reflected strong French influences, and it was decided to keep it secret, as Italy, Germany and the Netherlands had reservations about it. But the paper was, naturally, leaked, and condemned by Israel, who urged the Six to maintain a neutral attitude. The importance of the Schuman document was that it managed to unite the attitudes of the member states towards the Arab–Israeli conflict, and served as the basis for the EC's future attitude(s) towards the Middle East (Jawad 1992: 61).

In January 1973, Denmark, Ireland and the UK joined the EC. Their membership did not improve coherence. Traditionally, Denmark had a pro-Israeli attitude, building on respect for a people who had suffered more than most during the past centuries, with the German Holocaust as the height of its sufferings. This emotional attitude was strengthened by most Danish governments after World War II, being social democrat and having natural ties to the Israeli governments, which were labour for the first 30 years. Thus Danish prime ministers and foreign ministers made several visits to Israel during the 1960s, building, or rather keeping up, a good relationship between the two nations. But the Middle East was not an important topic in Danish foreign policy until 1973.

Ireland being a fairly 'remote' European country with a very limited foreign political activity until her membership of the EC,[8] did not have an official position on the Middle East. In spite of a sympathy for Egypt during the 1956 Suez action (rooted in the traditional Irish anti-British and anti-colonialistic attitudes), it would be wrong to label Ireland's attitude towards the Middle East as clearly 'pro-Arab'; it would be better to describe it as absent (Keating 1984).

The UK has had a long presence in the Middle East, including the protectorate of Palestine, but, contrary to France, the UK's Middle East policy has been somewhat ambivalent and inconsistent. On the one hand, the UK supported Arab unity in the 1930s, on the other hand it was Lord Balfour who promised the Jews a homeland, and the UK tried to find a solution by creating an Israeli and an Arab state in today's Israel. The alienation of Israel from the UK had its roots during the 1930s and went on during the short war of independence, during which the UK decided to get out of Israel. The ambivalence in UK Middle

8.   Ireland first became a member of the UN in 1956.

East policy was even more visible in the Suez action, when Israel, France and the UK together provoked Egypt and the Arabs. In spite of the Suez action, the UK was able to re-establish and keep good relations with especially the conservative Arab states, though public opinion in the UK supported Israel during the Six Days War.

Apart from historic involvement, the UK's motives for engagement in the Middle East before 1973 were similar to the French: trade and access to energy. Like France, the UK was interested in securing stability in the region, but also working for the containment of the Soviet Union. Geoffrey Edwards (1984: 48) has characterized British Middle East policy as: 'Britain has often appeared to leave it to others to take the lead, being content, seemingly, to remain in the middle of the pack'.

Thus, at the outbreak of the Yom Kippur War of 1973, the EC was divided in three blocks; a pro-Arab block (France, Italy), a neutral block (Belgium, Ireland and perhaps the UK, which tended to be pro-Arab), and a pro-Israeli block (Denmark, Germany and the Netherlands). This grouping has to be taken with caution, as many of the states had perceived interests in the Middle East, but not (yet) formulated real policies. Perhaps only France, Germany and the UK could be said to have some kind of Middle East Policy. This is important, as the three great powers of France, Germany and the UK disagreed on the question of how to approach the Middle East.

Table 4.1 schematizes the attitudes of the six original EC member states towards the Middle East complex at the time EPC began working in 1970, bearing in mind the dangers inherent in simplification.

Table 4.1: Attitudes of the EC member states towards the conflicting parties around 1970

	Pro-Arab	Neutral	Pro-Israel
Belgium		x	
France	x		
Germany			x
Italy	x		
Luxembourg[a]			
The Netherlands			x

a. Luxembourg did not have a Middle East policy at that time but being a small state it traditionally advocated solving conflicts through peaceful means according to international public law.

The EEC and the Middle East 1969–1973
As mentioned in the previous chapter the EC member states as well as
the EEC had important trade relations with the Arab states before 1973.

> The European Community's exports to Arab countries increased consi-
> derably after 1968 to reach $13.2 billion in 1974, accounting for 48 per
> cent of the total imports of the Arab League countries. During the same
> period, the share of EC exports to the Arab market increased steadily
> from 6.2 per cent in 1968 to 9.2 per cent in 1974 (Jawad 1992: 6-7).

Thus there were trade incentives to strengthen relations. Still, the Community lacked a clear strategy towards the Arab states, concerning trade
relations until 1972 (Jawad 1992: 7). In October 1972 at the Paris
Summit, the EEC adopted their so-called 'Global Mediterranean Policy'
(GMP), which was in fact not so much a global policy, as a framework
for bilateral relations between the EEC and the single Mediterranean
states.

> It was primarily a commercial strategy, aiming to facilitate the freedom
> of movement of industrial products. The GMP foresaw a preferential
> treatment for a limited number of products, which would enjoy tariff
> reductions from 20 to 80%, depending on the product. Limited financial
> aid was also included in the form of protocols (European Parliament
> 1999a: 16).

This framework was not entirely to the advantage of the non-EC states,
as they had to negotiate with the EC on an individual basis, thus
bringing their dependent situation very clearly to light.

Apart from the economic motives, one has to be aware of the GMP as
a part of the 1972 Paris Summit decision on strengthening the EC's
international role. Thus, the GMP must be seen as a part of establishing
a 'civilian power Europe' on the international scene. Jawad adds to the
economic motives three more: (1) through the 1960s the Soviet Union
had started to penetrate the Mediterranean region with a huge naval
build-up, at the same time as the defence-capability of the US was
brought into question; thus the EC sought to strengthen its ties with the
other Mediterranean states, with a long term aim of getting the
superpowers out of the region; (2) by the beginning of the 1970s the EC
was already aware of its dependence on a steady oil supply; and (3) the
integrational level of the EC had reached a point where the EC could
begin acting internationally (1992: 27-30).

The Period from 1973 until 1980

This part looks at the period from the Yom Kippur War (1973) until the Venice Declaration. It is the period when the Arab states experienced an increase in power and wealth because of their oil reserves which was unprecedented in their history and which would not last many years. This period also covers the formative years of the EC/EU's Middle East policy. The analysis will focus on four topics: (1) the oil crisis and its implications for the EC, internally and externally, and following that, the two policies which emerged from it; (2) the Euro–Arab dialogue (Gulf involvement); (3) the beginning of the EC/EU's involvement in the peace process; and (4) the Global Mediterranean Policy.

1. *The Oil Crisis.* Whereas the Arab attack on Israel came as a surprise for the nine EC member states, the following Arab oil war came as a further shock, in spite of the Commission's attempts to warn the member states. Before the Yom Kippur War only some of the member states had had a Middle East policy, now they all *had* to have one. What would be more natural than using the EPC to create a common Middle East policy and to show a united front? Not surprisingly this did not happen at first, although the interests in the region were fairly much alike. First of all, they were dependent on energy supplies from the region, and they thus had an interest in a stable region, both to secure the oil supplies and to prevent an escalation of a regional conflict into a global one. Secondly, the EC member states were interested in the region as a trade partner. Thirdly, they were interested in keeping the region as free of Soviet influence as possible; and fourthly, there were normative aspects both regarding Israel's right to safety and concerning Palestine's future, although the latter played only a minor role.

As mentioned above, OPEC placed an embargo on the EC. Furthermore, in a masterpiece of diplomacy OPEC effectively split the EC states, by categorizing them as 'friendly states' (France and the UK) where no sanctions were imposed; 'neutral states' (Belgium, Denmark,[9] Germany, Ireland, Italy, Luxembourg) where the 5% cut-back sanction was applied; and 'hostile states' (the Netherlands [and the USA]) where

---

9.   Denmark just avoided being classified as a 'hostile state'; the Prime Minister had declared that: 'In my view the Arab countries started the present war and I'd be willing to defend the aggressiveness of Israel to a large extent—for the neighbours of that country would like nothing better than to have Israel pushed into the Mediterranean' (Thune 1984: 80).

a total boycott was imposed (Jawad 1992: 65). Because of the relative failure of common attempts, each state had to manage as well as it could, thus demonstrating the lack of willingness to cooperate and a falling back to the traditional 'nation-state-alone-in-the-world' attitude.

At the end of October 1973 French President Pompidou asked the EC states to act collectively, and the result was the 6 November EPC Declaration on the Middle East, which marked the shift towards a French inspired, pro-Arab attitude. The declaration built on UN Security Council Resolutions 242 (cf. above) and 338 (1973).[10] A peace treaty should build on the following principles:

> (i) The inadmissibility of the acquisition of territory by force; (ii) The need for Israel to end the territorial occupation which it has maintained since the conflict of 1967; (iii) Respect for the sovereignty, territorial integrity and independence of every State in the area and their right to live in peace within secure and recognized boundaries; (iv) Recognition that in the establishment of a just and lasting peace account must be taken of the legitimate rights of the Palestinians (*Bulletin of the EC* 10, 1973, reprinted in Ifestos 1987: 610).

The declaration interpreted the UN Resolutions in a rather pro-Arab way, for example, by referring to the 'legitimate rights of the Palestinians', a phrasing until then used only by Arab states, but it also brought up two topics that the Israeli government had rejected discussing previously: (a) that Arab–Israeli negotiations should take place with a UN framework, and (b) that an international agreement should include international guarantees (Greilsammer and Weiler 1984: 134-35). Jawad writes about the declaration:

> It was viewed by the Arab side as a satisfactory response and a positive attitude towards understanding Arab demands in the struggle with Israel. The statement signalled a new era in Arab-European relations and was later to pave the way for the birth of the Euro–Arab dialogue (1992: 56).

Thus, the declaration did not fail to achieve its goal as the reaction came a few days later from an Arab summit in Algeria. First, it launched an appeal to the EC stating that Europe: 'was linked to the Arab countries across the Mediterranean by deep affinities of civilization and by vital interests which could not be developed except in a situation of trusting and mutually beneficial co-operation' (EC Commission 1982: 28). Secondly, the end of most of the oil embargo was

---

10. Resolution 338 repeated the essence of Resolution 242.

declared though the Netherlands was still to be boycotted in spite of being one of the Nine signing the declaration. Israel was disappointed about the turn of the events. Indeed, Israel's experiences with her European 'friends' had been a rather disappointing story. Abba Eban, foreign minister, declared that the statement meant 'Oil for Europe' and not 'Peace in the Middle East' (Greilsammer and Weiler 1984: 135).

Shortly after the 6 November EPC Declaration the EC heads of state and government met for their regular summit in Copenhagen in December 1973. Denmark had joined the EC on 1 January the same year, and had held the EC presidency since July. Just after the beginning of the meeting, an Arab delegation of Ministers turned up to deliver a message from the Arab countries,[11] a rather unconventional step. During the meeting, France and Britain successfully advanced the idea of creating a 'special relationship' with the Arab states, although it was unclear what exactly it should imply (Jawad 1992: 80). In the communiqué from the summit, two things of importance are mentioned: (1) the declaration of 6 November was reaffirmed, and (2) there was a call for entering into negotiations with the OPEC countries (EC Commission 1982: 28): 'their Heads of State and Government attached great importance to opening negotiations with the oil producers on overall arrangements including a wide range of co-operation…'.

Once more French diplomacy had had a victory. This French diplomatic victory has to be seen against the background of the US initiative for creating a 'consumers' front against the OPEC states, which was launched the day before the Copenhagen Summit, an action France was against. In spite of this, the rest of the EC member states were to follow the call of the US, but the summit declaration made it possible to follow a double track strategy. Thus the oil crisis[12] can be seen as the catalyst for two of the EC/EU's important Middle East policies: the Euro–Arab dialogue, and the involvement in the peace process (the Global Mediterranean Policy had been working since 1972).

11. A Danish civil servant present in Copenhagen has told one of the authors about the complete surprise of the fairly unexperienced President-in-office. 'All of a sudden some Arab ministers turned up in their white gowns, demanding to see the Heads of State and Government; what the Hell should we do? We gave them a cup of coffee, told our Minister, and they were admitted. Seemingly not all Heads of State and Government were as surprised as we were'.

12. See Jawad 1992 for a detailed account of the oil crisis.

The oil crisis also revealed the nature of the power relationship between the US and her European allies. The US had several interests in the Middle East, among others: to secure Western (i.e. US) influence in the region by keeping the Soviet Union out; to protect Israel from eradication; and to secure a stable supply of energy. The best way of securing these, at times contradictory aims, would be to secure a stable peace in the region. Thus the Yom Kippur War and the following oil crisis did not work in favour of US interests.

In Washington it was decided that the best way of solving the 1973 War was to work for peace within the UN framework and support Israel diplomatically and with weapons. As for the oil crisis, it was decided to create a consumers' front under US leadership, as mentioned above. This was fairly easy, as the USA was relatively independent of energy supplies from the Middle East. However, the situation was quite different for the Europeans, where 60% of the total energy need came from the Middle East (Jawad 1992: 68-69). France was hostile to the US idea which it considered very risky, and most other EC member states were sceptical. Still, the pressure from the USA was large and the EC states consented to participate. Ifestos quotes Lieber for observing: 'Secretary Kissinger and the US successfully exerted pressure for linkage between a continued American military commitment to Europe and the acceptance of American leadership on energy policy' (1987: 424).[13] The Europeans were not left in doubt who was deciding.

2. *The EPC and the Middle East Peace Process until 1980.* Apart from the Euro–Arab dialogue and the Global Mediterranean Policy, nothing much happened concerning the EPC's involvement in the Middle East between November 1973 and June 1977.

In the USA, President Carter had taken office in January 1977. Carter launched what he called a 'comprehensive approach' trying to settle all problems in the Middle East instead of taking the Nixon–Ford administrations' 'step-by-step approach'. Both President Carter and his Secretary of State Vance met all Arab and Israeli leaders during their attempts to bring about a favourable climate for negotiations. During this US initiative, the European Council met in London in June 1977, and issued a statement on the Middle East conflict.

---

13. See also Jawad 1992: 102-109.

In the declaration (*Bulletin of the EC* 6 [1977]: 62, point 2.2.3) the Council welcomed all efforts to bring an end to the conflict, and urged all involved parties to join and support the process. The Council then proceeded to repeat its statement from November 1973, word by word. What made this statement 'a landmark in the evolution of European attitudes' (Ifestos 1987: 441), came under point 3:

> The Nine have affirmed their belief that a solution to the conflict in the Middle East will be possible only if the legitimate right of the Palestinian people to give effective expression to its national identity is translated into fact, which would take into account their need for a homeland for the Palestinian people. They consider that the representatives of the parties to the conflict including the Palestinian people must participate in the negotiations in an appropriate manner to be worked out in consultation between all the parties concerned. In the context of an overall settlement, Israel must be ready to recognize the legitimate rights of the Palestinian people: equally, the Arab side must be ready to recognize the right of Israel to live in peace within secure and recognized boundaries. It is not through the acquisition of territory by force that the security of the States of the region can be assured; but it must be based on commitments to peace exchanged between all the parties concerned with a view to establishing truly peaceful relations.

Compared to the 1973 Declaration, the European Council in London went further concerning the rights of the Palestinian people, supporting them and identifying the Palestinian problem as the core of the conflict as well as giving less importance to secure Israel's borders (Greilsammer and Weiler 1984: 138). The declaration also embraced Carter's approach both concerning a 'comprehensive approach' (the EC spoke of an overall settlement), and concerning 'a homeland'[14] for the Palestinians.

President Anwar Sadat's subsequent unexpected trip to Jerusalem meant a return to the step-by-step approach, blocking Carter's initiative for a comprehensive agreement, as Sadat's initiative primarily was aimed at constructing peace between Egypt and Israel.

The French attitude towards the Sadat initiative was rather reserved to start out with, but later changed in such a way that all members of the Community could, and did, support Sadat with a common statement on 22 November 1977. Khader (1984: 170-71) comments that the

14. Ifestos (1987: 441) draws attention to the 'homeland' being the same as that used in the Balfour Declaration of 1917 that laid the foundation for today's Israel.

attitude of the EC was ambivalent; on the one hand they did not want to embarrass President Sadat's initiative, but on the other hand they were afraid of losing sight of a comprehensive peace agreement. It is worth noting that the Community slowly had come to adopt the French points of view concerning the Middle East, including the Palestinian problem. When Sadat's initiative ended in the signing of the Camp David agreement (September 1978) and subsequently the Egypt–Israeli Peace Treaty (March 1979), the Arab countries were outraged, and excluded Egypt from the Arab League.

In spite of initial French reservation about the Camp David agreement, the EC expressed its lukewarm support of the agreement, congratulating the three involved parties, urging the other Arab states to take a constructive stand by participating in the peace process but also reminding the parties of the many outstanding problems to be solved. Still, the basically supportive attitude was repeated in the communiqué of 26 March 1979:

> In this context they [the Nine] take due note of the will expressed by the signatories to the treaty to consider this not as a separate peace but as a first step in the direction of a comprehensive settlement designed to bring to an end thirty years of hostility and mistrust (Khader 1984: 171).

3. *The Euro-Arab Dialogue until 1980.* The Euro–Arab dialogue[15] was, as mentioned, born in Copenhagen, and its first and most constructive phase began with a joint Euro–Arab ministerial meeting in Paris, in July 1974, and it ended when the Camp David agreement was signed by Egypt and Israel in 1979, and Egypt subsequently was expelled from the Arab League. Several problems had prevented a swift start; the Commission's 1982 paper on 'The European Community and the Arab World' mentions two problems, and it does so in rather vague phrases (EC Commission 1982: 28-29): first, the US suggestion of a consumers' front, and secondly, the demand of the Arab League to allow the PLO to be represented in the talks.

The US plan for creating a 'consumers' front' ran counter to the European (French) plan. The aims of the USA were twofold; first to establish a strong consumers' front, preventing one state being played against the other by OPEC, and secondly, to reaffirm itself as the leader

15. A good account of the Euro–Arab dialogue is given by Haifaa Jawad (1992), despite occasional normative tendency.

of the West. On the other side France wanted to establish a dialogue with the Arab countries, both to secure energy supplies for Europe, and to present the EC as a third 'force' in the Middle East. In the end, the USA exerted so much pressure on Europe (e.g., by linking EC participation in the US project with USA's security guarantee for Europe), that all EC member states (apart from France) joined the process, which at a later stage led to the creation of the International Energy Agency (IEA). As a consolation to France, the rest of the EC member states decided to implement the dialogue with the Arab states.

The second problem was the participation of the PLO. When the idea of a Euro–Arab dialogue was launched the PLO, of course, existed, but that in itself was not a problem. The problem came as the October 1974 meeting of the Arab League which recognized the PLO as the sole representative of the Palestinian people, and as such the Arab League's 21 or so members. Consequently, the League demanded that the PLO should participate in the Euro–Arab dialogue. After some time, the 'Dublin Compromise' was reached. Instead of one delegation per country participating, there would be two groups, an Arab and a European one; each group could itself decide whom to send to the meetings (EC Commission 1982: 29).

Ifestos (1987: 434-35) mentions a third problem for the Euro–Arab dialogue, which does not figure in the Commission's report from 1982, namely the constant Arab attempts to politicize the dialogue. To avoid too many problems, the EC decided from the outset to exclude the two most explosive topics: oil and the Middle East conflict. The strong Arab condemnation of the EC–Israeli association agreement of May 1975 was linked to this problem, nearly jeopardizing the planned Cairo meeting. It took some diplomatic effort before the problem was solved. This time the EC was not willing to give in to Arab complaints (Jawad 1992: 94-96). The dialogue began and was at a later stage (1976) officially institutionalized with the General Committee as the highest organ (although the identical structure had existed since the Paris meeting of 1974 (Khader 1984: 168). It was to meet twice a year at ambassadorial level. Equally seven working parties and a time schedule for their work was agreed (EC Commission 1982: 30).

Within the EC, the Euro–Arab dialogue was coordinated by a special inter EPC–EEC working group, reporting to both the COREPER and the Political Committee of the EPC. It was the first time that the boundaries were broken down between the EEC and the EPC; such proceedings were institutionalized with the Amsterdam Treaty about 20 years later.

The first meeting in Cairo 1975 was important for the further development of the EC–Middle East policies, including the Venice Declaration. In a joint declaration, which was written into the charter of the Euro–Arab dialogue, *inter alia* the following points were mentioned (EC Commission 1982: 29):

> (a) The Euro–Arab Dialogue is the product of a joint political will that emerged at the highest level with a view to establishing a special relationship between the two groups.

> (b) The Dialogue's political dimensions are in essence the attempt to rediscover, to renew and to invigorate the links that affect these neigh-bouring regions; the desire to eliminate misunderstandings that gave rise to difficulties in the past; and the intention to establish the bases for future co-operation, embracing a wide area of activities, to the benefit of both sides. The growth and flourishing of Arab–European economic co-operation should proceed on this understanding which will contribute towards stability, security and a just peace in the Arab region and towards the cause of world peace and security.

> [(c) ...]

> (d) In the field of economics in particular, the Dialogue aims at establishing co-operation capable of creating the fundamental conditions for the development of the Arab world in its entity and of lessening the technological gap separating the Arab and the European countries. This necessitates the seeking of effective measures and steps in all domains based on an equitable division of labour between the two groups.'

This declaration points to two aspects of the Euro–Arab relationship: (1) The EC wished to create a 'special relationship' with the Arab world, and (2) based on a diffuse 'common cultural heritage' the economic character of the relationship is stressed. The importance of economic aspects is seen from the fact that six out of seven working groups which were set up in Rome 1975 were related to economic and social questions, and one to cultural questions (EC Commission 1982: 30).

In spite of the Arab states' attempts to bring up the Arab–Israeli conflict, the EC succeeded in keeping political topics off the agenda both in Luxembourg 1976, and in Tunis 1977 where the Arabs pressed especially hard. Especially in Tunis 1977, the Arab side emphasized both the paramount importance of dealing with all aspects of the Euro–Arab dialogue, including the Arab–Israeli conflict, and the need for the

EC to recognize the PLO. The EC delegation promised to consider these wishes. Contrary to the meagre political result, the Tunis meeting was able to note progress within nearly all fields of economic co-operation (Jawad 1992: 124-30).

As mentioned previously, the work of the Euro–Arab dialogue was suspended in April 1979 as a consequence of the Camp David agreement which had established peace between Egypt and Israel in March 1979 and gained the support of the EC for this process. This Arab step of suspending the Euro–Arab dialogue showed with clarity that the Arab League did not consider the 'special relationship' with the EC that valuable after all. The EC had not been willing to turn the dialogue into such a political forum the Arab states had wanted, and worse still from an Arab viewpoint, the EC had not recognized the PLO. Perhaps the final factor which made the Arab states decide to suspend the dialogue was that the EC insisted on Egypt's continuous participation in the dialogue.

In the time after the suspension of the dialogue, the EC member states tried to revive the Euro–Arab dialogue. At the meeting of the EPC in September 1979, it was decided to attempt a renewal of the dialogue (Khader 1984: 168). At a series of meetings between the EC president-in-office and the secretary general of the Arab League, attempts were subsequently made to find common ground for relaunching the dialogue. During these talks it turned out that the Arab side insisted on including political aspects in the talks, if they were to be restarted (EC Commission 1982: 34).

Ifestos summarizes the European experiences in three points: first, the Europeans succeeded in avoiding a complete breakdown of the dialogue until Camp David; secondly,

> As regards economic, trade and energy questions, the results…may have been meagre, but, on the other hand, it may be regarded as a damage-limitation exercise at a period of rising energy prices, high political demands from the Arab side, and a growing importance of the Arab market because of its oil revenues; (1987: 438)

and thirdly, the whole exercise gave the EC a possibility to show itself off as an international actor, with a certain success.[16] All together, one can claim that the Euro–Arab dialogue served the European interests as

---

16. Jawad disagrees with this positive assessment, but does so from an Arab influenced starting point (1992: 159-60).

well as one could expect under the given circumstances. This was the situation leading up to 'Venice 1980'.

4. *The Global Mediterranean Policy until 1980.* As mentioned above the EC endorsed its Global Mediterranean Policy in October 1972, and it concluded its first association agreement under the Global Mediterranean Policy with Israel in 1975, very much to the anguish of the Arab states. The aim of the agreements was to set up free trade and economic cooperation between the two sides. The EC–Israeli agreement included three main points:

> [1.] In the industrial sector, the agreement provided for the progressive dismantling of all tariff and quota barriers... [2.] In the agricultural products, the Community made enormous tariff cuts covering about 85 per cent of Israel's agricultural exports to the Community, mainly traditional products such as citrus fruits and fruit juice. [3.] The agreement moreover contained other areas of co-operation such as the stimulation of investment, exchange of technical knowledge, and Israeli participation in scientific and technical ventures between the Nine and the other non-member states (Jawad 1992: 94-96).

The joyful reactions from the Israeli side and the equally sour reactions from the Arab side clearly show how impossible it is to separate trade and politics The reaction of the Israeli foreign minister was that 'a trade deal which could bring the Arabs and the Israelis together within the framework of a common policy would be most helpful economically, psychologically, and politically' (Jawad 1992: 96). This suggestion implies, first, that Israel contributed an active and positive role to the EC in the Middle East; secondly, that Israel sought peace; and thirdly, they basically had some of the same ideas which underlay the later Barcelona Process.

Two years after Israel's agreement with the EC, Egypt, Jordan, Lebanon and Syria signed similar agreements, in spite of their initial reluctance.[17] Thus, this part of the EC Middle East policies can be said to be a success. The main reason is that the discussion of the Arab–Israeli conflict has not been included in it (this does not imply that political topics have not been touched upon: the European Parliament froze the Third and Fourth Financial Protocol with Syria due to her violations of Human Rights: European Parliament 1999a: 24).

17. Other agreements were signed with Cyprus, Malta, Portugal, Spain and Yugoslavia (Gomez 1998: 135).

As mentioned previously the non-EC states were not fully happy about the GMP, and for a reason. The GMP had not succeeded in reducing the disparity between the EC and the GMP-associates: 'By 1979 the aggregated trade deficit of the Mediterranean associates with the Community stood at 9 billion ECU compared to 4 billion ECU in 1973, while export growth actually slowed down' (Gomez 1998: 136).

5. *Summing Up.* Just after the oil crisis had broken out, one could summarize the attitudes of the individual states towards the Middle East conflict as shown in Table 4.2.

Table 4.2: Attitudes of the EC member states towards the conflicting parties after the oil crisis

	Pro-Arab	Neutral	Pro-Israel
Belgium		x	
Denmark			x
France	x		
Germany		x	← x
Italy	x		
Ireland		(x)	
Luxembourg		(x)	
The Netherlands			x
United Kingdom		x	

Looking at the same table at the end of the 1970s would reveal that Denmark, Germany and the Netherlands had toned down their support for Israel, at least in public.

Panayiotis Ifestos, an expert on EC–Middle East relations, sums up the effects of the oil crisis on the EC (1987: 421):

> It [the oil embargo] made Europeans brutally aware of their vulnerability in both economic and political terms; it changed the pattern of relationships with both Israel and the Arab world, and brought about a dramatic shift towards more pro-Arab attitudes; it revealed the extent of European external disunity and generated calls for more integration as a result of this experience; it had economic effects not imaginable before the crisis; and, last but not least, it brought to the surface the uneasy nature of Euro-American relations.

Another attempt to distill a 'European position' was undertaken by Greilsammer and Weiler (1984: 123):

At its simplest the position would suggest a solution to the conflict (essentially the Palestinian dimension) whereby Israel would return the West Bank and Gaza (the Territories), in which an independent Palestinian state probably led by the PLO would be created, in exchange for recognition of, and 'security guarantees' for, the Jewish state.

All other attempts to solve the Arab–Israeli conflict would have to be measured against this position, and would have to comply with it to gain European support.

The EC and the Middle East from 1980 until 1989

Let us briefly look at the 'road to Venice'. Several factors made it clear for the EC that a European peace initiative was needed. First, at the end of the 1970s and the beginning of the 1980s the Middle East as a region had become even more unstable. Adding to the Arab–Israeli conflict, the Gulf region had changed character becoming a region of instability and internal crisis. The fall of the Shah of Iran (1979), the outbreak of the Iran–Iraq War (1980), the rise of Islamic fundamentalism, and the Soviet invasion in 1979 of Afghanistan (lying close to the region) clearly showed this. Seemingly, the EC could not count on the assistance of the US as 'policeman' in the region, to protect its interests. Secondly, the Camp David agreement previewed a solution of the Palestinian problem but, as it turned out, Egypt and Israel could not agree on it. Also, the USA exhibited a lack of willingness to press for a solution. The result was Arab disappointment, and a turning towards the EC as a possible way of exerting pressure on the USA (Ifestos 1987: 451-52). Thirdly, internally, the EC had gained more experience in presenting a united front—although there were many lapses—and thus the EC felt capable and ready to play a role; now its vital interests were at stake.

During the summer of 1979 the EC declared that a comprehensive agreement was needed to make peace possible in the Middle East (June), and that it attached great importance to reassuming the Euro–Arab dialogue (September). In March 1980 the EC member states voted for a UN resolution condemning Israeli settlements in the occupied territories, and, among others, France, the UK and Germany made declarations in favour of the PLO (Greilsammer and Weiler 1984: 123). Collectively, the EC prepared an initiative containing three controversial parts (Jawad 1992: 219): first, to modify UN Security Council Resolution 242, by replacing the word 'refugees' with 'Palestinians';

secondly, to confirm the rights of the Palestinians to self-determination; and thirdly, to recognize the PLO as a legitimate representative for the Palestinian people.

The reaction to this initiative was not surprisingly positive in the Arab camp, and very negative in the Israeli camp. But the real pressure came from the USA where President Carter demanded that the Europeans wait, and basically to keep out of the peace process. President Carter stated:

> We are monitoring very closely what is being done by others, notably the European Community, to make sure that they don't do anything that would interfere with or subvert the progress of the Camp David procedure. We will protect the UN Security Council Resolution 242 with a veto if necessary (cited in Ifestos 1987: 457).

Jawad lists three reasons for this parochial attitude: (1) the US considered Camp David as the centre of the peace process, and anything which would endanger that would endanger the process; (2) the US believed that the Camp David process would create a positive spillover by itself; and (3) President Carter considered Camp David as a major asset in his re-election campaign, and thus he did not want the UNSCR 242 to be changed (1992: 221, see also Khader 1984: 172).[18] The EC once more yielded to US pressure, and when the meeting in Venice in June 1980 came, the declaration, although important in its own right, was much less controversial than it could have been.

The Venice Declaration was intended to establish the EC as a actor in its own right in the Middle East, but had been watered down owing to US pressure. The Declaration begins by repeating the previous EC statements including the support for UNSCR 242 and 338, and the right for all states in the region to live in security. The central parts of the declaration are points 6 to 9. In these parts three central issues are discussed: (1) the Palestinian problem (developing the lines from the previous declarations); (2) the status of Jerusalem; and (3) the question of the Jewish settlements (*Bulletin of the EC* 6 [1980]: 10-11, point 1.1.6):

---

18. Allen and Smith (1984: 187) draw our attention to the fact that the tension between the EC and the USA fits a pattern of transatlantic disagreements on the Middle East dating back to the Suez Crisis. To the Europeans the USA was too obsessed with the Soviet threat in the Middle East, as well as much too close to Israel to be able to play a constructive role.

6. A just solution must finally be found to the Palestinian problem, which is not simply one of refugees. The Palestinian people, we are conscious of existing as such, must be placed in a position, by an appropriate process defined within the framework of the comprehensive peace settlement, to exercise fully their right to self-determination.

7. The achievement of these objectives requires the involvement and support of all the parties concerned in the peace settlement which the Nine are endeavouring to promote in keeping with the principles formulated in the declaration referred to above. These principles apply to all the parties concerned, and thus the Palestinian people, and the PLO, which will have to be associated with the negotiations.

8. The Nine recognize the special importance of the role played by the question of Jerusalem for all the parties concerned. The Nine stress that they will not accept any unilateral initiative designed to change the status of Jerusalem and that any agreement on the city's status should guarantee freedom of access for everyone to the Holy Places.

9. The Nine stresses the need for Israel to put an end to the territorial occupation which it has maintained since the conflict of 1967, as it has done for part of Sinai. They are deeply convinced that the Israeli settlement constitute a serious obstacle to the peace process in the Middle East. The Nine consider that these settlements, as well as modifications in population and property in the occupied Arab territories, are illegal under international law.

With these statements, the EC clearly signalled its sympathy with the Arab side; stepping on all the bunions it could. The Israeli reaction was equally prompt and sharp. Prime Minister Begin compared the declaration with Adolf Hitler's 'Mein Kampf' and used the harshest possible language; ending by remarking that the value of the declaration was nothing:

> The decision calls upon us and other nations to involve in the peace process to bring in the Arabs' so-called PLO... For the peace that would be achieved with the participation of that organization of murderers, a number of European countries are prepared to give guarantees, even military ones... Anyone with memory must shudder, knowing the result of the guarantees given to Czechoslovakia in 1938 after the Sudetenland was torn from it, also in the name of self-determination... Any man of good will and every free person in Europe who studies the documents will see in it a Munich surrender, the second in our generation, to totalitarian blackmail and an encouragement to all those elements which seek to undermine the Camp David agreements and bring about the failure of the peace process in the Middle East (Greilsammer and Weiler 1984: 144).

The Venice Declaration had far-reaching consequences both for the actual EC–Israeli relationship, and for the ability of the EC to play a role as mediator in the Middle East. Peters states (1999: 299): 'The Venice Declaration marked a low-point in Israel's relations with the European Community from which it has never fully recovered'. President Carter rejoiced in the knowledge that the EC had given in to his wishes, stating that 'We have made good progress in staying the European allies from interfering in the Middle East peace process' (quoted by Jawad 1992: 226). The moderate Arab states welcomed the declaration, whereas the PLO's executive committee was not satisfied, as it did not go far enough. After a long critical survey of the declaration, it concluded:

> From the beginning, the PLO has entertained no illusions about the size of the European role, in view of the fact that this role has so far been associated with the US strategy... The PLO welcomes the move. However, it calls on the European states to take more independent stances and to free themselves of the pressures and blackmail of US policy... (in Ifestos 1987: 465).

In a way all the criticism and comments are right: the declaration did stipulate a rather insecure guarantee for Israel, it did not interfere with the Camp David agreement, and it did not go as far as to recognize the PLO as the 'sole representative' of the Palestinian people. But the declaration was also a fairly clear and stringent statement from nine individual states of their concern. As such it marks both a development towards a comprehensive European attitude towards the Middle East and it is a manifestation of the EC as a fairly independent international actor. This gives the Venice Declaration both an internal and external importance. Trying to explain why the declaration had fairly little impact on the peace process in the Middle East, one important reason was that two of the main parties (Israel and the PLO) were disappointed or directly negative towards the document.

1. *The Middle East Peace Process 1980–1989.* It goes without saying that the New Cold War (1979–85, see above) also spilled over into the Peace Process. It very much contributed to a polarization of the world around the two superpowers which did not appreciate too much foreign political activity from their allies. This superpower attitude was clearly shown when the European states wanted to take an initiative towards the Middle East, as seen above in relation to the US pressure exerted on

the EC concerning the Venice Declaration. At the same time, the Middle East itself was haunted by one crisis after the other, e.g., 1980–88 the Iran–Iraq War, disapproval of the Fahd Plan 1981, the assassination of President Sadat 1981, Israel's attack on an Iraqi nuclear reactor 1981 and bombings in Lebanon, Israel's invasion of Lebanon 1982, US raids on Libya 1986, the Hindawi Affair 1986 and so on.

The road forward from 'Venice' was expected to be at first one or two fact-finding missions to map out the political possibilities for a concrete European peace initiative. Gastorn Thorn, Luxembourg's foreign minister and president-in-office, went on the first of these trips to the Middle East in autumn 1980. He visited all relevant Arab and Israeli leaders to whom he explained the Nine's intentions, and listened to their reactions. Basically, the Arab side was more or less supportive, whereas the Israeli attitude was strongly negative (Greilsammer and Weiler 1984: 140-48). With the change of EC presidency, the Dutch foreign minister, van der Klaauw, also went on a similar mission to the Middle East in spring 1981. Before his trip, the pro-Israeli Dutchman declared (in Ifestos 1987: 477): 'the European Community submitted no proposals for a settlement of the Middle East conflict', and he declared that his trip was merely to work for mutual understanding and that he would stop in Washington to avoid any misunderstandings. The change of policy was rather clear; the traditionally pro-US and pro-Israel Netherlands, did not intend to deviate from its traditional affiliations while in office.

Van der Klaauw's above-mentioned idea of stopping in Washington was necessary. The new US President Reagan was by no means interested in any European 'interference' in the plans of the US concerning the Middle East. Reagan's administration had, contrary to the Carter administration, taken a global approach to US foreign policy, reflecting the major international problem, the New Cold War. All US foreign policy reflected the tensions between East and West, as did the US engagement in the Middle East. Thus, European initiatives that might jeopardize US overall strategy were not welcomed.

Therefore the auspices for a new European initiative were unfavourable, and they were perceived as such by the Europeans themselves. In the final statement from the European Council meeting in Luxembourg in June 1981, it asks the foreign ministers to continue working on possible EC peace initiatives, but generally it seemed as if the EC engagement in the Middle East Peace Process had 'run out of steam' (Ifestos

1987: 484). In the years to follow, the EC/EPC made no substantial collective initiative in connection to the Middle East, whereas France and other states pursued individual policies, although the EPC occasionally made statements on the Middle East.

Concerning the EC Middle East policy in the beginning of the 1980s Ifestos concludes that:

> The temptations of the early 1980s partly to substitute national approaches with a collective European position—or even common behaviour on the ground—gradually faded in view of changes which occurred in Europe, the United States and the Middle East region... This fact indicates that the efforts of Europe to develop a collective diplomatic behaviour, are easily influenced by both exogenous and endogenous developments; unlike national diplomatic behaviour which is comparatively coherent, common European diplomacy is fragile, very vulnerable to a number of factors, and easily reversible (1987: 501).

The Israeli invasion of Lebanon (June 1982) created a most tense situation in the Middle East. It stopped all on-going initiatives: the US efforts to solve the Middle East conflict by an international conference, the EC's preparations to issue yet another declaration, and Egypt's attempts to get the autonomy talks going. The EPC issued a strong, condemning statement, calling upon Israel to withdraw all troops immediately, otherwise the Community would consider the imposition of sanctions (Khader 1984: 176-77). At the European Council, held in France in June 1982, the Ten repeated the condemnation of Israel's invasion, but also showed that the Ten could not agree on what to do. Basically it was France unilaterally or together with Egypt, that was involved in the process. As Ifestos writes:

> Thus, while France was one of the principal external actors actively involved in an ongoing conflict, the Ten were discussing general and hypothetical questions about further meetings with undefined moderate Arab States to promote the troubled Fahd plan (1987: 510).

By 1983 the EC had limited its policy to supporting the Reagan Plan[19] and the Fez decision.[20] During 1984 the two European Councils

19. The Reagan Plan (September 1982) included the following points: (1) total autonomy for the West Bank and Gaza population in association with Jordan; (2) free elections of Palestinian authorities in these areas; (3) a freeze of Israeli settlements in the occupied territories; and (4) a gradual transfer of authority to the elected Palestinian authority.

20. 'The Fez decision of the Arab summit at Fez (Morocco, 6–9 September

supported and encouraged the dialogue between Jordan and the PLO, and also supported the Reagan and Fez plans. However, the words were not transformed into concrete initiatives; neither were they in 1985. The EPC rhetorically supported the peace initiative, but nothing more.

One central problem in the Arab–Israeli conflict was the question of mutual recognition. As long as Israel did not recognize the Palestinians' right to self-determination, the PLO would not recognize Israel, and furthermore, as the PLO refused to recognize Israel's right to existence, Israel would not recognize the PLO; a classic deadlock, where both parties were unable to take a first step (Greilsammer and Weiler 1984: 123-24 and 128-31). On the European side, it was especially France and the UK that individually tried to speed up the process and realized the importance of the recognition problem. A British initiative where a Jordan-Palestine delegation in London should recognize Israel's right of existence looked quite successful; but the attempt did not succeed. The EPC went on to support an international conference, dialogue, moderation and self-restraint. Basically, it was not until the end of the New Cold War in 1989 that the Community/EPC came up with a more substantial proposal, as will be seen in the next chapter.

'The positions and diplomacy adopted by the European Community throughout the 1980s did little to advance its ambitions of playing a significant role in bringing about a peaceful resolution to the Arab–Israeli conflict' states Peters (1999: 301). His reasons for this were that (1) the EC constantly reflected Arab points of view in its statements, thus preventing it from being taken seriously as a mediator by Israel, and (2) the EC had neither capacity nor influence over the conflicting parties to bring them to negotiate (1999: 300).

2. *The Euro–Arab Dialogue 1980–1989.* In addition to the above mentioned Venice Declaration, the heads of state and government declared their wish for a relaunch of the Euro–Arab dialogue at the same summit in Venice 1980. This wish was endorsed by the Arab

1982) stated that a solution of the Palestinian problem should provide for the withdrawal of Israeli forces to the 1967 borders, dismantlement of the settlements in Arab territories, guarantee of religious freedom in the Holy Places, Palestinian self-determination under their sole representative, the PLO, the establishment of a Palestinian state in the West Bank with Jerusalem as its capital, and United Nations Security Council guarantees "for all states in the area"' (Ifestos 1987: 414-15, n. 135; see also Khader 1984: 197-98).

states, but not by the US. According to Allen and Smith (1984: 189-90) this initiative was about to drive Dr Kissinger, then US Secretary of State, near to distraction. Dr Kissinger interpreted the dialogue as a successful Arab attempt to drive a wedge between the USA and the EC over the Middle East conflict. A number of preparatory meetings were held but in spite of the agreement to resume the dialogue (at the Brussels meeting in July 1980) nothing happened until the ministers met in Athens in December 1983.

Reasons for the postponement are many. On the Arab side internal disagreement was growing, fuelled by several other developments including the Iran–Iraq War, the peace plan of King Fahd (which was rejected by Syria, Libya, Algeria, South Yemen and the PLO), and the assassination of Egypt's President Sadat. As seen, the EPC in 'Venice' had agreed to send fact-finding missions to the Middle East. They did not make a very positive impact on the European Middle East process. On the contrary, according to Jawad (1982: 235), the second fact-finding mission in February 1981 constituted the start of a policy of delay and a change of attitude of the EC towards the Middle East. This change was reinforced by the shift of the French president, from the very pro-Arab Giscard d'Estaing to the more moderate François Mitterrand. Adding to this, the now ten EC member states decided to participate in the international peace-keeping force in Sinai, thus showing their support for the Camp David agreement.

Khader argues that the postponement of the Euro–Arab dialogue was inevitable (1984: 169): 'Europe was too hesitant and the Arab World too unpredictable'. When at last the Euro–Arab dialogue was resumed with the meeting of ministers in Athens in December 1983, it was a complete failure; the parties could not even agree to issue a final communiqué.

In spite of this failure, contacts were kept up between the Arab and the European sides, but they did not succeed in agreeing on the future of the dialogue. In the autumn of 1985 the Arab side tried to break the deadlock by suggesting a new meeting at ministerial level to discuss political matters. The reaction from the EC was positive, as long as it did not discuss specific political matters (i.e., the Palestinian question and the recognition of the PLO as sole legitimate representative of the Palestinian people). The Arab response to the European wishes was negative (Jawad 1992: 238-40). In spite of attempts to bring momentum to the dialogue, which almost succeeded in 1988 when a meeting was held in Bonn to prepare a sixth meeting of the General Committee, the two sides never succeeded.

Was the Euro–Arab dialogue a flop? Looking only at the list of concrete achievements and all the aborted summits, the answer must be yes. But if one looks a bit more cynically at it from a Euro perspective, the dialogue was a modest success. As a means of *Realpolitik* the dialogue secured the EC several advantages: (1) it created a reasonable relationship with the Arab world in a period of crisis, and helped establish the EC as a factor (albeit a minor one) in the Middle East, which would be of importance in the new millennium; (2) it constituted a forum for learning collective diplomacy; and (3) it paved the way for the EC–Gulf dialogue (see below). For the Arab side, the main political benefit of their dialogue was to have it as a showpiece for the USA (and the Soviet Union); though fairly early in the process it became clear to the Arab states that the dialogue would not give them the political forum they needed. To the Arab side, the dialogue was still there as a symbolic alternative to the USA. Thus, it helped to blur the cruel reality in the Middle East that the single most important Middle East power was and is the USA, as long as it wishes to be so. At a more concrete level, the Euro–Arab dialogue helped in making the PLO acceptable, insofar as the EC member states were quick to recognize the PLO as indispensable in the peace process. It is also worth noting that the Euro–Arab dialogue can be seen as one of the forerunners of the Barcelona Process, and as such has a value of its own.

3. *EC–Gulf Dialogue.* While the Euro–Arab dialogue was suspended, and finally died, the EC felt a strong need for creating relations with the Gulf states,[21] in order to secure stable trade relations, as they counted for more than two-thirds of the EC export to the Arab countries and could 'recycle' their 'petrodollars'. The EC wanted to make this approach along the lines of the Global Mediterranean Policy. A hindrance to a European initiative was that the Gulf region had become very unstable. Thus, the EC also had to work for stability in the region, especially as the EC had learnt that it was not enough to count on the assistance of the US as 'policeman' in the region.

---

21. The Gulf states are Bahrain, Kuwait, Oman, Qatar, Saudi Arabia and the United Arab Emirates (UAE).

In spite of the cold Euro–Arab relationship Germany tried to launch a new dialogue in December 1979, but was unsuccessful; neither the EC nor the Arab side were interested (Jawad 1992: 184-86). The Arab side had two concerns: they did not want only to talk economics, separate from the Arab–Israeli conflict, and they were afraid of the possibility that a separate dialogue could divide the Gulf states from the rest of the Arab states. A year later in 1981 the six Gulf states founded the Gulf Cooperation Council (GCC). The GCC had economic tasks, as well as political ones. Shortly after the founding of the GCC, the EC initiated informal talks with the aim of creating a cooperation agreement. The talks had their ups and downs, and first ended in 1988 after long and often complicated negotiations, when the GCC accused the EC of conducting a protectionist policy, as the EC did not want to conclude a free-trade agreement. Finally, in June 1988, a cooperation agreement was signed in Luxembourg. The parties agreed to cooperate in the following fields: economic affairs, agriculture and fisheries, industry, energy, science, technology, investment, environment and trade (Jawad 1992: 168-204).

The EC initiative towards the Gulf states demonstrated a number of important points: first, it underlined the dependence of getting steady oil supplies from the Gulf; secondly, it stressed the need to gain access to the lucrative Gulf state markets; thirdly, it showed the lack of confidence in the ability of the 'Free World's Leader'—the USA—to help its allies and secure stability in the Gulf; fourthly, it marked the end of the EC paralysis, which found its role as international actor; and fifthly, it showed that the Gulf states enjoyed priority over the rest of the Arab states and the Global Mediterranean Policy.

4. *The Global Mediterranean Policy (GMP) 1980–1989.* The GMP also suffered from the crisis in the 1980s, and in spite of its 'technical character' it was used politically, for example, when the EC decided to exclude Libya from the programme after the accusations of support of terrorism hardened in 1986.

The European Parliament's working paper 'The Middle East Peace Process and the European Union', summarized the situation in the 1980s:

> The non-EC Mediterranean countries were not fully satisfied with the Global Mediterranean Policy. As the agreements were signed bilaterally, they allowed for variations in the extent of preferences on industrial

goods, in the restrictiveness of agricultural trade provisions, in aid and technical assistance and so on. Moreover, they were aware that their level of commercial dependence on the EC made them vulnerable to economic decisions taken in Europe. This became evident in the 1980s, when the preferential access of agricultural and industrial products was limited by the accession of Spain and Portugal to the European Community in 1986 and by the workings of the Common Agricultural Policy (European Parliament 1999a: 16).

Thus, the Arab states were ready for 'something more' at the end of the 1980s, something which manifested itself in the Barcelona Process (Gomez 1998: 138-46).

In the pre-Barcelona phase the EC often had problems in formulating and especially implementing the GMP. Internal and external pressures were at work. Gomez (1998: 138) mentions three reasons for this. First, the EC's internal policies set limits as to how many concessions it could make. Secondly, members of the Council of Ministers were clearly aware of how far their domestic basis would allow them to go. Thirdly, the EC was limited by external actors. Still, the creation of the GMP in 1972 showed that the EC had a belief in its own power to manage a common economic policy in the region, as well as provide hope for a positive, predictable development in the region for all states (Waites and Stavridis 1999: 22). Thus, the main importance of the GMP, as in the case of the Euro–Arab dialogue, must be seen as helping to create a relationship between two interlinked, but distinctively different, regions, Europe and the Middle East. The Barcelona Process would probably not have proceeded had not the GMP and the Euro–Arab dialogue existed.

5. *Summing Up.* The period began with the 1980 Venice Declaration which signalled the eagerness of the EC to play an active role in the Middle East. The declaration was received with hostility from Israel, reluctant appreciation from the Arab side, and relief from the USA. It was meant as a platform from which the EC should develop a genuine Middle East policy. As it turned out, Venice fulfilled neither European nor Arab hopes. Already after a year, the EC's initiative had vanished, and for the rest of the 1980s, the EC's collective Middle East role was virtually non-existent, although Arab countries often tried to mobilize support from the EC.

Still, the long-term importance of the Venice Declaration is not to be underestimated:

it was the Venice Declaration of June 1980, issued one year after the
signing of the peace treaty between Israel and Egypt, which marked the
emergence of a distinct and common European stance towards the Arab–
Israeli conflict and outlined a collective position on the steps to be taken
for its peaceful resolution. Sixteen years later, the Venice Declaration
still constitutes the basic principles of European policy towards the Peace
Process (Peters 1999: 298).

As previously mentioned neither the internal nor the external environment was to the EC's advantage when considering the possibilities
of playing an active role in the Middle East. Internally, the change of
French President also changed the French attitude towards the Middle
East. This, together with the EC's Mediterranean policy, and the negotiations leading to the European Single Act, absorbed a lot of energy,
giving the EC's foreign political approach a lame and uncertain air.
Externally, the USA put heavy pressure on the EC not to interfere, a
pressure which was strengthened by the outbreak of the New Cold War
in 1979, making the Allies rally around the colours of the leader of
NATO. Adding to this, the Middle East 'exploded' in the first half of
the 1980s, thus polarizing the parties. Altogether the real possibilities
for a genuine political role were small (see below).

The economic approach to the region went reasonably well, seen
with European eyes. The Global Mediterranean Policy and the Euro–
Arab dialogue in its EC–GCC version also went fairly well. In spite of
various troubles, the EC succeeded in keeping these relations afloat,
and developed. They laid the foundations for the Barcelona Process of
the 1990s.

*The European Community as an International Actor in the Middle East
1969–1989*
Recalling Sjöstedt (cf. Chapter 1), an international actor needs two
qualities: autonomy and capability. Autonomy implies that the unit is
discernible from its environment, and that it has a minimal degree of
cohesion. This condition was fulfilled already at the Hague summit in
1969, albeit in a fragile manner. The visibility of the EC/EPC progressed steadily in the period 1973–89, owing to the declaratory policy
of the Community, stating that it wanted to be an international actor,
speaking with one voice, and owing to its coordinated gravity or
presence (Allen and Smith 1990) in the economic field; it had to be
taken account of. Thus, the first quality of an international actor was
there; the second quality, the actor capability—the 'unit's capacity to

behave actively and deliberately in relation to other actors in the international system'—was not developed to the same extent. This creates Christopher Hill's (1993) famous 'capability–expectation gap' implying that the EC itself, as well as some of the outside actors, actually expects it to be able to do more than it actually can. Sjöstedt's structural prerequisites (1977: 74) only developed to a rudimentary degree during the period in question.

The whole period can be considered as a learning process for the EC member states, whereby they began developing a community of interests as well as a goal articulation system, especially concerning the Middle East, and during which they collected quite a fund of experience and knowledge. However, resources were at a fairly low level; within certain areas they were virtually non-existent as were decision-making and monitoring facilities. The very loose structure of the EPC clearly was a handicap, whereas the EC decision-making process worked well (for example, in the GMP). Equally underdeveloped was the so-called 'action performance instruments' of the EPC which should have included a network of agents and transaction channels, but did so only in a very fragmented way.

Sjöstedt insists that being an international actor is not the same as being, for example, a superpower. 'Actorness' is a quality which can vary in strength. The EC began developing this quality in 1969, and the Middle East was one of its first cases. The 'hey-day' of EC/EPC Middle East policy was the middle of the 1970s until the end of the 1979, or the beginning of the 1980s. The outside world believed in the EC capability, more than the EC member states did themselves. That created frustration especially in the Arab world, which at the beginning had seen the EC as some kind of counterbalance to the superpowers' presence in the region. The European Community was able to be active in the period when détente was working but, as soon as the New Cold War broke out, the role of the EC diminished.[22] Thus, the EC had learnt that the USA expected to be recognized as leader (united consumers' front), but also that the USA was not able to protect the interests of the EC outside Europe (e.g. in Iran). The EC was basically absent when important decisions were made concerning the Middle East. But, the Community was able to create a network of low politics agreements,

22. This pattern endures. The EU tries to be active now after the end of the Cold War, thus implying that in times of international crisis superpowers have less patience with their minor allies than in times of peace.

thus paving the road for the reconciliation which came in the 1990s. This was not an illustrious and heroic role, but still an important one. Adding to this, the experiences of others deciding matters of importance, as well as witnessing one's own impotence, helped fuel the integration process within the EC itself, paving the way to the Single European Act, the Maastricht Treaty, the Amsterdam Treaty, the Helsinki Decision and the Nice Treaty.

The European Union and the Middle East 1989–1991

Change in International Relations
The purpose of this section is to present an outline of the developments in international relations that occurred between 1989 and 1991 and redefined the nature of international relations. The main efforts will be devoted to a discussion of the implications of these events for Europe and the Middle East, concluding with an assessment of the Community's relations to the Middle East. The second step will explain the reasons that led to the Second Gulf War, that is, Iraq's occupation of Kuwait, and the implications for Europe, and the Middle East and their relations.

1. *Changes in the Soviet Union.* In December 1991, the Soviet Union was dissolved and replaced by the Commonwealth of Independent States and an epoch had come to an end. From a European perspective one of the consequences of the demise of the USSR was that the changing political climate paved the way for the opportunity to unify Germany.

The new Germany became the most powerful state in the EC, and there was increasing concern of how to ensure that German interests were oriented towards the West, and not the East. In other words, the anxiety over a united Germany, the security implications over the collapsed Soviet Union, and the fear of a US military withdrawal from Europe were strong forces for further integration. With regards to Germany, the concern over Germany's international orientation was further amplified in the light of Germany's reaction towards the unfolding crisis in Yugoslavia which became a major challenge for the EC/ EPC. The EC argued in favour of the integrity of the state, but Germany leaned on the EC to recognize Slovenia and Croatia as independent states.

2. *Post-Cold War Implications for the Middle East.* The demise of the Soviet Union had serious implications for its Arab allies as it left them politically and economically vulnerable in four important ways. The political backing, military assistance and economic aid which had been flowing since the 1950s dried up and the changing situation forced the regimes to evaluate their policies—international, regional as well as domestic. First, the possibility for the Arab states to manoeuvre in the bipolar setting, extracting the highest policy gains from the super-powers had disappeared. Secondly, the Arab world soon found itself competing with Russia and Eastern Europe for foreign aid and other external resources from the EC and the USA. Regarding the conse-quences for the so-called Soviet clients, Iraq, Syria, South Yemen and the PLO were those most immediately affected. In order to find foreign backing South Yemen turned to Saudi Arabia, whereas Syria and the PLO sought to improve their relations with the USA. Iraq, as it later became apparent, went its own way. Some would argue that Israel was perhaps most affected by the influx of nearly half a million Soviet Jews who had to be absorbed and integrated (Yapp 1996: 500). Thirdly, the Arabs believed that the US bias in favour of Israel was strengthened in the wake of the Soviet emigration and there was grave concern that any settlement in the Arab–Israeli conflict brokered by the USA alone would favour Israel. Fourthly, regarding the definition of 'the enemy' in international relations, there was a fear that the disappearance of the threat of Communism would create the incentive for 'the US creation of a functional equivalent to the Soviet threat in Arab nationalism or Islamic fundamentalism...both of which have symbolic currency in the West as harbingers of international terrorism' (Karawan 1994: 435-36). Clearly, with the gradual Soviet exit there was indeed 'no counter-vailing power to constrain or inhibit direct US intervention in the Middle East' (Karawan 1994: 434). In sum, in the late 1980s the influence of the USSR was on the decrease in the Middle East. The USSR had instead chosen to cooperate with the US as a junior partner in regional issues.

The Gulf War

In addition to the uncertainty over the developments in the Soviet Union, Saddam Hussein was preparing a move which was to have serious ramifications in international relations. On 2 August 1990, Iraq invaded Kuwait. There were several reasons motivating the invasion:

- the unsolved question of Iraqi debt to Kuwait for the oil supplied during the Iran–Iraq war;
- the claim that Kuwait was exceeding its OPEC quota which had a damaging effect on Iraq's economy;
- the right to the Rumayla oilfield;
- the right to possession of the Kuwaiti islands of Babiyan and Warba which were important for the development of Iraqi port facilities;
- the old Iraqi claim to Kuwait;
- after the failures in the Iran–Iraq War, Saddam Hussein was eager to secure a foreign policy victory and repair his damaged image (Halliday 1991: 225).

The following day, the Arab world condemned the Iraqi move, but calls for negotiations and withdrawal soon failed. On 29 November 1990, the UN Security Council issued an ultimatum: Iraq would have to leave Kuwait by 15 January 1991, or face the consequences. As the message was ignored, a multilateral force gathered in Saudi Arabia initiated an air offensive on 17 January and on 24 February they launched a ground attack with the aim of evicting Saddam Hussein from Kuwait.

The intervention was successful in that the Iraqi forces were expelled from Kuwait and Iraq's bid for regional hegemony was averted. The ground war had weakened, but not destroyed Saddam Hussein, and even though thoughts of disposing him had circulated, it was hoped that an internal coup would oust him from power. It soon became clear that the sanctions later imposed on Iraq by the international community had no direct effect on the regime, and the chances of a successful coup attempt were reduced by the hour as Hussein rebuilt his position. Uprisings in the south of the country were crushed, but the Kurds succeeded in obtaining the promise of UN guaranteed 'safe havens' in the north of the country (Burkay 1997: 465).

1. *The Arab World and the Gulf War.* From an Arab perspective, the Iraq–Kuwait crisis was primarily a bilateral conflict. Sayigh (1991) argues that the Iraqi invasion was made possible because the structures and rules determining the Arab regional order had broken down. The national policies of the Arab states were not reflecting any particular interests towards collective regional stability and security, nor state security, but rather reflecting the personal interests and narrow-minded ambitions of the Arab leaderships. The period between 1967 and 1975 saw the peak of Arab solidarity and cooperation and even the reluctant

mutual recognition of fellow Arab states. It was the time when Saudi Arabia acted as the financial sponsor for countries like Syria, Egypt, Jordan and several others. The defining interest and first priority during the period was the Arab–Israeli conflict and, in relation to this, it was also the period in which the PLO was recognized as the sole representative of the Palestinians, as mentioned. The advent of the oil revenues post-1973 further enhanced cooperation and the funds available. However, the Sinai II agreements and the Camp David accord led to Egypt's isolation within the Arab world. Later, the invasion of Afghanistan, the Iranian Revolution and the Iran–Iraq war destabilized the regional balance, and marked the end of the regional solidarity and the basis for establishing new alliances between the Arabs. Following this, it was then domestic interests and policies that became the prime determinant of the nature of external relations, and not regional concerns (Sayigh 1991: 497).

The 1980s have been described as the decade of missed opportunities. At the turn of the decade, the Middle East had access to enormous financial resources. It is impossible to identify one single reason for the series of failed opportunities. However, one could argue that it was the domestic power structures and the systems for the (uneven) allocation of wealth, which was instrumental to the waste. Of equal importance was the system of control whereby the regimes could engage in co-option of the social forces, brutal oppression of the opposition or instead seek to establish a middle ground. This pattern was also reflected at the regional level where the oil-producing countries used their oil wealth to further their own interests, either by paying for the loyalty of their potential opponents (bribes), or supporting their allies. With the virtual absence of accountability to and dependence on their local constituencies, the recipient governments could engage in hefty spending on military and internal security programmes when the external funds they received would be used as compensation within the national economies (Sayigh 1991: 499). The *rentier* policy, concentrating wealth among the few, insulated the regimes from demands for reform. The oil revenues were also used in a religious context with the support of conservative Islamic groups throughout the region. The money was used to fund mosques, cultural centres and political movements like the Muslim Brotherhood in Jordan, the Hamas in the Occupied Territories and the Algeria Islamic Salvation Front (Sayigh 1991: 501).

In spite of their wealth, the Arabs found themselves facing an economic crisis in the late 1980s. As the flow of external funding began to dry up, the economic mismanagement and over-spending which had fuelled national debts, also made it more difficult for governments to control internal civil dissent peacefully. Although several Arab states were facing national as well as inter-state conflicts of various kinds, there were no joint efforts to ease tensions, as long as there were no threats to the regional *status quo*.

During the late 1980s, the Iran–Iraq War was at its most ferocious and, furthermore, Israel and Iraq were trading insults and exchanging threats of chemical attacks. There was concern over European integration which, from an Arab perspective, could have negative implications for migration, trade and economic relations with the Maghreb (North Africa). Moreover, the Soviet Union was in the process of withdrawing politically and militarily from the region. It was in this context that Kuwait and the United Arab Emirates broke ranks by exceeding their OPEC quota and forcing prices down. This move damaged Iraq's economy, which was at a critical junction just after the end of the Iran–Iraq war in 1988. As the Arab world already had been put to the test with famine, economic crises and civil wars, there was no particular interest from the Arab states in deterring an Iraqi invasion of Kuwait. With the clarity of hindsight it was to be expected that there would be a need for external intervention (Sayigh 1991: 501-503).

2. *The Result of the War.* As well as being restored as a state, Kuwait abandoned its deference to Arab nationalist rhetoric and reliance on Arab neighbours for security as a result of its liberation. Instead, a US–Kuwait security agreement indicated a strong preference for a US military presence, and reliance on the US for security. As regards relations with Kuwait's immediate neighbours, Iraq had been seriously weakened, but had remained intact as a state. Still, the unpredictability and presumed hostility of Saddam Hussein made any hopes for a stable region unrealistic. In spite of its fierce anti-US stance, Iran had remained remarkably silent throughout the conflict, but had, according to Hudson (1992: 302), emerged as the major Gulf power and the new hegemon of the Gulf. Yet, Saudi Arabia also emerged as a winner after the Iraqi defeat, especially after regaining control of the oil market, though the security of the Saudis at that time depended on the relationship with Iran.

Egypt joined the UN coalition in the liberation of Kuwait and, although Egypt was later rewarded financially by Kuwait and Saudi Arabia, it appeared that the hoped-for reconstruction contracts and the anticipated compensation for the jobs lost both in Kuwait and Saudi Arabia were not to materialize. Yet, victory for the USA in the Gulf could improve the chances of a US-led effort to obtain a peace settlement in the Arab–Israeli conflict. Even if the result would only be acceptable for the Palestinians and Arab opinion, this benefited Egypt's security and thus ultimately Mubarak's prestige (Hudson 1992: 304).

> The Syrian leadership engaged in verbal acrobatics to legitimize its alignment against Iraq, an alignment which yielded economic assistance from the Gulf Co-operation Council countries (GCC), improved relations with the US, and allowed for more political influence in Lebanon (Karawan 1994: 444).

In brief, Syrian President Hafiz al-Asad had managed to shift his policies from the Cold War dependence on the Soviet Union and advocacy of Arabism to a more pragmatic course which entailed a greater dependence on the US—without antagonizing the other Arab states. This change in relations coupled with the impression that the US had moved closer to the Syrian position vis-à-vis the peace process were some of the reasons why Syria attended the Madrid Conference in 1991.

For Jordan, the war and its aftermath became a disaster, which in seriousness was only equalled by the loss of Jerusalem and the West Bank in 1967. Jordan, which had expressed sympathy with some of Iraq's views and advocated an 'Arab solution' to the crisis, suffered economically under the sanctions imposed on Iraq, Jordan's main market. Furthermore, the difficulties in absorbing more than 300,000 refugees from Kuwait, Saudi Arabia and Iraq also strained the cohesion of the kingdom to breaking point (The Economist Intelligence Unit 1996: 18). For the PLO the Gulf War forced the leadership to assume a more pragmatic approach and greater separation of PLO interests from the Arab interests in general (Karawan 1994: 447).

3. *Other Consequences of the War.* It is impossible to assess the exact number of casualties in the war and its aftermath. Some estimates are as high as 100,000 Iraqi military deaths and 3000 civilian casualties. Yet the numbers of deaths in the Shi'ite and Kurdish uprisings are even more uncertain.

Some of the implications of the war were that the intervention in Iraq fuelled an anti-Western/anti-US feeling in many parts of the region. There were widespread frustrations that the adherence to international law was applied selectively and the Palestinian problem and Israel were not subjected to the same attention, and this showed the insincerity of the West. Some argued also that the intervention was part of a larger US plan to maintain control over the region; humiliating the Arabs and demonizing Saddam Hussein was merely a ploy to justify a continued military presence in the region (Azzam 1991: 484).

Another implication was that the Kuwait crisis was the final *coup de grace* to any notion of Arab unity. The Arab world had been unable to solve the tensions internally—in other words, to find an 'Arab solution', for example through the Arab League. Instead they decided to align with an external power against a fellow Arab state. It was generally recognized by the 1960s that Arab nationalism had failed and this had paved the way for a more prominent role for the Islamist discourse in Middle East politics. This trend had thus been in the making, but Islam's profile became more visible in the post-Gulf War and post-Cold War era. Since the power of the religious movements increased, it soon became a necessity for the regimes and the secular political movements to adapt to the terminology of the Islamist discourse. Lastly, as mentioned, the end of the inflow of the external resources meant that the Middle East economies became more vulnerable since the demographic developments made the system unable to keep up the pace and forced the government into further debt.

The European Approach to the Gulf War and its Aftermath
The hopes of seeing the Gulf War as the catalyst for the EC to transform itself into an international actor were disappointed. The war clearly demonstrated how the separation of defence and security, the EPC domain, from the external relations of the EC limited the functionality of the Community in international relations, especially in times of crisis. The EC did manage to coordinate diplomatic actions and impose economic sanctions on Iraq. But the contributions to the war effort itself offered by the member states were symbolic and put into effect without much coordination (Nugent 1994: 393). The main European contribution to the war came from Britain, which quickly aligned itself with the US line. It was only after failed unilateral, diplomatic efforts to solve the crisis that France joined the coalition, while

Spain advocated military action. Officially, Germany was prevented constitutionally from participating militarily, but contributed financially to the US costs instead. The rest of the Community members contributed symbolically and in a more piecemeal fashion. The then President of the European Commission, Jacques Delors, was under-standably one of the first to express his disappointment at the EC/EPC level of performance—he was also partially blamed for raising general expectations too high for the EC to achieve as an international actor. It is necessary to bear in mind the limited institutional capacity of any intergovernmental framework and, furthermore, the EPC's limited resources when assessing the real efficiency of the performance during the Gulf War. One could argue that the EPC did indeed act to the best of its abilities, but the expectations, internally as externally, towards the potential capabilities of the EC had been raised too highly—among other things with talk of a potential Common Foreign and Security Policy.[23]

The Gulf War motivated the EC to assess its policies towards the Mediterranean and the Middle East. The existing protocols with the Mediterranean countries were to expire in 1992 and were therefore to be renegotiated. One of the priorities for the EC was to ensure that cooperation between the Mediterranean and the Middle East countries would be improved through a framework for political and economic cooperation in order to prevent similar conflicts from occurring in future. As the war was unfolding, one dimension of the European debate focused on the creation of a Conference on Security and Co-operation in the Mediterranean and Middle East. The proposal was tabled by Italy but rejected by the Council of Ministers in 1991, shortly after the end of the War (Aliboni, Joffé and Niblock 1996: 123-24). However, some progress was made in other fields. The EC had actually launched its 'New Mediterranean Policy' in December 1990. The new initiative was 'intended to reinforce existing trade and aid agreements with support for economic reforms such as liberalization and structural adjustment' (Hollis 1997: 23). The proposal meant that the EC would support cooperation in the Mediterranean through 'technical coopera-tion, feasibility studies of regional infrastructure projects, and educa-tional and research activities' (Aliboni *et al.* 1996: 123-24). Between

---

23. This dilemma was summed up in an article on the 'expectations/capability gap' of the EC (Hill 1993).

1992 and 1996, the EC would commit 4.5 billion ECU and a further
300 million ECU to the southern Mediterranean countries, earmarked
as compensation for the adverse effects of structural adjustments.
Furthermore, relations between private southern Mediterranean enter-
prises and EC companies would receive support and the market access
for Mediterranean agricultural products would be improved. It was
within the Mediterranean policy framework that small-scale projects
were set up, such as the Mediterranean Environment Technical Assistance Programme (METAP), MED-Invest, MED-Campus and MED-
Media. The latter three belong under the Trans-Mediterranean Network
Agency (Aliboni *et al.* 1996: 123-24). In these programmes it was
emphasized that initiatives including more than one country as well as
those which benefited the environment would generally be preferred.
Although the 'New Mediterranean Policy' clearly marked a step forward in the EC policies towards the region, the resumption of the
negotiations on the Arab–Israeli conflict in 1991 was soon to inspire a
further reassessment and fine-tuning of the policy.

Summing Up: The EC and the Middle East 1969–1991

The frame of our analysis—the international system—changed character several times in the period treated by this chapter, thus changing
the EC member states' freedom of action. It began as a loose bipolar
system leaving ample space for the smaller Western actors to conduct a
foreign policy of their own choice, as long as they accepted that there
were two camps, an Eastern and a Western, and that the US was the
leader of the Western. Détente was succeeded by a system of tight
bipolar character, the New Cold War from the end of the 1970s until
the end of the 1980s. This tight bipolar system was characterized by the
EC member states being under US tutelage. The superpower rivalry
hardly left room for dissenting opinions. This situation in return helped
strengthen the position of those EC member states that worked for the
possibility to play an independent role, shaping their own future. The
next phase was introduced by the fall of the Berlin Wall in 1989 and
was confused for the first few years. The question was whether the
international system had turned multipolar or unipolar. The messy state
of affairs gave many states in the international system a feeling of
freedom of action, hitherto unprecedented, and the period coincided
with the negotiation of the Maastricht Treaty on European Union as

well as the Gulf War. The end of the Gulf War can be seen as the end of the transition phase of the Cold War. It became rather obvious that one would have to consider the international system as unipolar with the US as unrivalled hegemon, although there were a number of potential pretenders *inter alia* China, Russia, India and the European Union. Thus an international system of a multipolar character is not an unlikely scenario in the long term.

As mentioned, the CFSP's predecessor, the EPC, took off during détente and developed in the fairly loose bipolar system. It gained sufficient strength to develop further during the New Cold War (e.g. the Single European Act) in spite of, as well as due to, the strict discipline of the USA. The fall of the Berlin Wall in 1989—a sign that the Soviet empire was cracking—triggered off the negotiations leading to the Maastricht Treaty in 1992.

No superpower has been able to exercise full control over the Middle Eastern states, but they have been able to use their respective client states in pursuing their global interests as well as to protect 'their' states from annihilation. On the other hand, the Arab client states have been successful in manipulating their 'patron state' into supporting them in conflicts which did not fit into the two superpowers' activities. The EC engaged itself in this game from 1970 onwards.

The activity of the EC has been divided in two categories in this chapter; the economical, mainly supranational part (EC) and the inter-governmental, mainly EPC, part. The economic 'low politics part' has developed quietly, with ups and downs, but basically benefiting the interest of the EC all the way to 1991. The political 'high politics' part was set off by the oil crisis of 1973 and resulted in nearly a decade of active EPC involvement in the Middle East, where the EC/EPC tried to play a role as 'third party' beside the USA and the USSR. The initial involvement of the EC was welcomed by the Arab states, but they soon realized that the EC did not have the capability to outweigh the USA or the USSR. This became clear to all involved parties around the time of the Venice Declaration in 1980, when the USA successfully exerted strong pressure on the EC. Times had changed, and the New Cold War was waging. During the rest of the decade, the EC kept a low profile in high politics. The active involvement in the Middle East high politics came with the Gulf War, when some EC member states participated vigorously, but others did not. It all, of course, happened under US leadership.

It is clear that the 1980s and the first year of the 1990s were not glamorous for the EC. Before judging the decade one has to remember that the New Cold War and the international system's tight bipolar structure did not allow the EC many possibilities for an active, alternative policy and, secondly, that the EPC was not geared to conduct the large-scale foreign policy of a superpower. Keeping these restrictions in mind, another picture emerges when trying to evaluate the EC's performance, and it is clearly positive. The EC was able to formulate a common policy on a complex issue, and it was able to implement the 'low policy' part of it. The 'high politics' part taught the EC valuable lessons on how to conduct collective foreign policy, and it clearly demonstrated to the member states the shortcomings of the EPC system, thus laying the ground for the CFSP.

The EC foreign policy actions 1969–91 prepared the ground for the Madrid and Barcelona conferences in the 1990s; thus the EC did make a difference and it had a part in what could be termed the 'decade of hope' which followed.

5 |

The European Union and the Middle East in the Post-Cold War Era

From the 1991 Madrid Conference until the 1995 Barcelona Conference

After the Gulf War: The Start of the Peace Process

From a Middle Eastern perspective, the Gulf War had increased the sense of strategic vulnerability of nearly all actors in the region. The Gulf states had been forced to call for external intervention, and Iraq's Scud-B missile attacks on Israel had challenged the perception of the Occupied Territories as a security asset and strengthened Israel's belief in the necessity of curbing Arab weapons of mass destruction. Also, the PLO had been weakened by the war, as previously described (European Parliament 1999a: 26).

After the war the USA had confirmed its position as the sole remaining superpower. The Bush Administration sought to use its influence and the momentum from the Gulf to establish a framework for negotiations, which could lead to a comprehensive peace agreement between Israel and her Arab neighbours. With the USSR as co-sponsor, the US succeeded in convening with the Middle Eastern states a conference in Madrid in October 1991. The subsequent negotiations were to become 'the peace process', or the 'Madrid peace process' (Hudson 1996: 334-35). The parties invited were delegations from Lebanon, Syria, Jordan, Palestine, Egypt and Israel. The UN, the Gulf Cooperation Council and the EC were in attendance, but only as observers. The Madrid Conference resulted in a 'two track' process—a bilateral and a multilateral.

The purpose of the bilateral track was to establish a framework for negotiations between Israel and Jordan, Israel and Lebanon and Israel and Syria. The Jordanian delegation was initially formed as a joint Jordanian-Palestinian delegation due to Israeli demands (Jensen and Laursen 2000: 30-31). This meant that Israel and Jordan were to negotiate a settlement of the Israeli–Palestinian conflict without the PLO—instead Palestinian negotiators were included in the Jordanian delegation. Politically, Arafat and the PLO were seriously weakened in the aftermath of the Gulf War, as Israel knew, and Arafat had no alternative but to accept the conditions for the negotiations. It was only later that the Palestinians separated from the Jordanian delegation. The initial negotiations—as the subsequent negotiations—were to focus on issues such as territoriality, borders, security and the rights of the Palestinians. In essence, the purpose of the bilateral track was to solve the regional problems, which stemmed from the past (Beyerle 1998– 99). The role of the USA was to act as a 'neutral' broker and facilitator.

The response of the European Community to the Gulf War itself had been considered inadequate and stimulated the drive for further integration within the EC. The Gulf War 'provided an object lesson—if one were needed—on the limitations of the European Communities' (Delors 1991: 99). Furthermore, the EC had announced that it would present a European peace initiative after the end of the war. It hardly came as a surprise that the EC initiative was abandoned as the interests and initiatives of the member states were too divided; Britain and Germany supported the US peace initiative, whereas France wanted an initiative based on the principles of the Venice Declaration (European Parliament1999a: 26). Some would argue that the situation in Eastern Europe and the USSR, the emerging crisis in Yugoslavia, and the plans for further integration led the Europeans to the conclusion that at that time resources were best spent joining the US-led initiative in Madrid. At the conference, the Dutch presidency presented the EC position, which remained the demand for the observance of the UN Security Council Resolution 242 and 338. The EC also argued that the Arabs should end the trade boycott of Israel, and that Israel should halt the settlement activities in the Occupied Territories and withdraw from Lebanon (European Parliament 1999a: 27-28).

The results of the bilateral peace negotiations were slow in coming. In 1992, however, Israel's new Prime Minister Yitzhak Rabin signalled a willingness to consider concessions in relations to the Golan Heights and ordered the freezing of some settlements in the Occupied Terri- tories, which at first improved the climate for negotiations. However, the expulsion of Islamic activists to Lebanon only months later compli- cated the situation and eventually led to a deadlock in the negotiations. It also soured relations with the EC with whom Israel was lobbying for an upgrading of the 1975 cooperation. In the peace process there were no firm results until September 1993 (Hollis 1997: 20).

The purpose of the multilateral talks was to create an international forum where regional issues of a technical and/or practical nature would be debated by experts in working groups, that is, issues such as water, environment, refugees, arms control and regional security, and regional development cooperation. Naturally, some issues could ultimately only be solved by political decisions, but the aim of the working groups was also a logical consequence to serve as confidence building measures (European Parliament 1999a: 28-29). The EC received an important position in the multilateral track as so-called gavel-holder (or chair) of the Regional Economic Development Working Group (REDWG) (Beyerle 1998–99). The purpose of the REDWG was to support the establishment of intra-regional economic ties and the establishment of institutions, which would enhance the possibilities for economic cooperation. Between 1993 and 1997 the EU allocated $15.2 million for the preparation of feasibility studies of infrastructure and the establishment of communication networks between cities, universities and media (European Parliament 1999a: 28-30). In general the result of the working groups have been modest, and as a reaction to the suspension of the Israeli–PLO negotiations by Israeli Prime Minister Netanyahu, the Arab countries froze the process of normalization with Israel and reintroduced the boycott.

1. *The Declaration of Principles (DoP).* The Declaration of Principles was signed in Washington DC in September 1993 by Yitzhak Rabin and PLO leader Yasser Arafat (Maksoud 1995: 117). The Declaration of Principles was a mutual recognition of Israel and the PLO, and a framework for a future settlement, which consisted of three stages: first, Israeli withdrawal from Gaza and Jericho; secondly, the arrangement for Palestinian self-government (the Palestinian Authority); thirdly, a final status for the Occupied Territories, to be negotiated (Declaration of Principles, Annex 9, European Parliament 1999a). As the bilateral negotiations had come close to collapse in 1992, there had been secret negotiations taking place in Norway, and it was this secret channel which led to the agreement.

At the Washington Donors' Conference, convened on 1 October 1993 the international community pledged $2.4 billion in donations to the Palestinian economy. The hope was that the financial injection could contribute to the development of the Occupied Territories and the raising of the living standards of the Palestinians, and improve the environment for foreign investments. After the signing of the Declaration of Principles, Israel and the PLO continued the negotiations and the efforts to apply the DoP. The first results were two agreements signed in Cairo in 1994. The first agreement signed in February focused mainly on the question of control of international borders and Israel's control of settlements in Gaza. The second agreement in May established the conditions for Israeli redeployment and the setting up of a Palestinian police force. It has sometimes been referred to as the 'Gaza-Jericho, First'. In response to the deal, the EC donated 10 million ECU to the establishment of the Palestinian police force (European Parliament 1999a: 33).

2. *Jordan and Israel: The Peace Treaty.* Jordan was shocked over being kept in the dark with regard to the negotiations over the DoP and was seriously concerned about the long-term effects of the DoP on Jordan's internal situation and over Jordan's position in the region (Jabarwi 1995: 101-102). However, as the PLO was the first to break ranks in this post-Camp David process, it paved the way between Jordan and Israel in 1994 for a full peace treaty. The treaty was in itself a serious attempt to normalize relations, politico-economic as others, between the two countries (Salibi 1998: 275). It was hardly surprising that Syria condemned the treaty since it feared being sidelined in the negotiations and losing bargaining power vis-à-vis Israel as the other Arab states concluded their agreements. The EU expressed its support for the treaty, but was not involved in its creation.

3. *The Taba Agreement/Oslo II.* The Taba Agreement, signed in September 1995, was one of the most important post-DoP agreements between Israel and the Palestinians. 'The agreement provided for the expansion of the geographical borders of the Palestinian self-government on the West Bank and the election, for the transition period, of a Palestinian Council which would be vested with legislative and executive powers' (European Parliament 1999a: 35). This being said, the transfer of authority to the Palestinian Authority was not complete. The territories were divided into categories (A, B and C) over which Israel retained varying degrees of control. The West Bank was 'atomized', that is, divided into geographically separate cantons, and it was merely

fragments of lands, not necessarily with any geographical connection, which were now under the authority of the Palestinian Authority. The policy of land division, some argue, resembles most of all the Bantu-stan policies of South Africa's apartheid era (Jensen and Laursen 2000: 51).

4. *The Case of Iraq.* In 1993, the Clinton Administration presented its 'dual containment policy' (Shirley 1994: 1). The European position was that the 'dual containment' policy, which in brief was an economic boycott of Iran and Iraq, would only serve to antagonize further the opposition in the two countries and further complicate relations to the West. The usefulness of the policy was questionable, to say the least. The EU developed the 'critical dialogue', which was less confrontational than the US approach, and permitted long-term relations to be maintained (read: safeguarded European strategic economic interests). Nevertheless, both approaches have so far failed to yield any serious results (Shirley 1994: 7). Between 1991 and 1995 there was a general consensus that the UN and EU sanctions against Iraq were to be upheld pending Iraq's compliance with UN demands to eliminate all programmes for the development of weapons of mass destruction and long-range missile capabilities. UN Security Council Resolution 986 permitted Iraq to sell oil in order to purchase medicine and food, but the process was to take place under strict UN supervision. The bone of contention between the Western allies centred on the conditions and timing for the lifting of the sanctions (Hollis 1997: 27). In the aftermath of the war, France, together with the UK, conducted naval patrols in the Gulf and air surveillance over Iraq in order to monitor the country, but also to act as a military deterrent for Iran. The UK and France also held military exercises with the GCC countries, notably Saudi Arabia. This was, however, done neither in cooperation, nor coordination with the USA. With regard to the sanctions, France argued that the lifting of sanctions depended on verification from the UN that Iraq had complied with all demands.

With intense competition in the Far East and only modest markets in Africa, many European businesses regard Iran and Iraq as potentially lucrative markets once the sanctions are lifted (Serfaty 1998: 3). France has maintained links with the Iraqi business community, though not doing business they were 'stealing a march' on their European competitors. The UK was more ambiguous, arguing that sanctions would only be lifted when Iraq could be trusted, that is, when Saddam Hussein was evicted from power. Yet, UK businesses were prevented legally from dealing with Iraq (Hollis 1997: 27-28). In sum, on Iraq it appeared that the UK was closer aligned to the US position than was France, who stood closer to the European foreign policy line.

The Europeans and the Gulf Cooperation Council (GCC)

The institutional framework behind the Community and the GCC was established by a cooperation agreement in 1988, which came into force in 1990. A Joint Council of EC–GCC foreign ministers was to meet on a semi-annual basis to discuss matters of mutual interest, and Technical Working Groups were formed to deal with the details (George 1998a: 32-33). The aim of the relationship has been to strengthen the economic and the technical cooperation between the EC and the GCC, and support development and diversification of the GCC economies. The way of achieving the aims were by varying degrees of economic cooperation where the end result should ultimately be a free trade agreement between the two parties (Saleh 1999: 1).

From a European perspective, the interests in relations with the GCC are based on the fact that the GCC represents the fifth largest market for manufactured exports and that it remains the most important supplier of oil to Europe (COM (95) 541/2.1). For Europe, a closer partnership with the GCC provides the EU, first, with an ally who may function as broker between the EU and other Middle Eastern states or Iran, and, secondly, with an ally with interest in keeping open the shipping routes and, generally, in stability of the region. According to Saleh, the EU seeks to enhance 'cross-investment' since GCC investments in Europe would increase the interests in a well-functioning European economy, which ultimately is extremely sensitive to fluctuations in oil prices. European Union investments in the GCC states would help the diversification of the economies and decrease the dependence on oil prices (Saleh 1999: 1-3).

There are several reasons why results have not been forthcoming in the relationship. First, the inability of the GCC to unify its tariff structures, which the EU had demanded before substantial talks on a free trade agreement could be initiated. Secondly, the European proposals for a reduction of CO_2 emissions by a carbon tax have been met with opposition (Saleh 1999: 11). Thirdly, the EU has continuously sought to protect its own refining industries from the more sophisticated Gulf products and has consequently been reluctant to open markets (Hollis 1997: 26). However, there have been some results primarily in the organization of conferences, symposiums and workshops on issues such as cooperation on energy, environment and industry mainly focusing on boosting private sector initiatives. Also, the GCC opened a mission to the EU in 1994 (George 1998a: 32-33). Still, the relations never developed as intended between 1990 and 1995 and criticism intensified. Therefore, in 1995 it was decided to postpone the Joint Council meeting and instead call for an EU GCC Troika Ministerial Meeting, the purpose of which was to breathe new life into the cooperation. This was regarded as a turning point in relations as the focus was shifted from the potential free trade agreement to a strengthening of political and economic cooperation (Saleh 1999: 15).

Reviewing the Situation: Preparing for the Barcelona Conference
The relative progress of the peace process created a further impetus for the EC to refine its approach to the Middle East and North African countries in the post-Cold War era. Moreover, from a Middle Eastern perspective the European '1992' single market project led to concerns over a 'Fortress Europe', as said, and prompted calls for a revision of the existing bilateral agreements. It was in the process of negotiations both within the EC and between Europe and the Middle East and North African countries that new ideas and concepts emerged which were gradually incorporated into the discourse that resulted in the Euro-Mediterranean (Euro-Med) Partnership Initiative[1] which was launched in 1995. In 1992 and 1993, the Council of Ministers adopted two documents which outlined the EC's interests in the Middle East and North Africa (Aliboni *et al.* 1996: 124-25). The EC would promote bilateral political and economic cooperation between the member states and the Mediterranean countries, which should pave the way for regional cooperation and integration at a later stage. The cooperation was to be aimed at supporting socio-economic development and job creation in the Mediterranean countries, which ideally would curb the influence of Islamic movements and limit the chances of labour migration to Europe—two central concerns of the EC (Aliboni 1996: 30). Moreover, the extreme population growth in the region was also

---

1.   See http://www.euromed.net for the Euro-Med Partnership website.

regarded as a crucial issue to bring under control, since it hampered efforts by placing increasing demands on society and not least on Europe because of migration (Parfitt 1997: 870). Also worth mentioning is that the 1993 document defined for the first time 'the Middle East' (the Arab *Mashreq*) as Egypt, Syria, Lebanon, Israel, Jordan and the Occupied Territories. It was then to be considered separately from the North African countries, the *Maghreb* (Aliboni *et al.* 1996: 124-25). Initially, the EC interests were focused on the Maghreb countries and particularly on Morocco. The EC strategy, which took shape during 1992, was to negotiate partnership agreements within a common framework for the Maghrebi countries with an increasing focus on free trade. This was to be organized within the 5 + 5 formula (Algeria, Libya, Mauritania, Morocco and Tunisia from the southern Mediterranean and France, Italy, Malta, Portugal and Spain from the northern Mediterranean) (Selim 1997: 70-71).

Although Spain was perceived as one of the driving forces within Europe it was Morocco which brought the concepts of 'free trade' and a 'Euro-Mediterranean space' into the discourse. Over the following two years Tunisia, Israel and Egypt also approached the EC calling for bilateral free trade agreements, which supported the trend (Gillespie 1997: 37). Egypt, who commenced negotiations with the EU in 1994, in the post-Cold War era sought to diversify its foreign policy options, among other things, by enhancing relations to the EU *qua* the emerging Euro-Mediterranean framework. Egypt was not included in the 5 + 5 negotiations and the Egyptian proposal for a 'Mediterranean Forum', which was to promote socio-economic and technical-scientific cooperation and cultural dialogue was understandably 'a deliberate attempt to water down the 5 + 5 formula and replace it with a pan-Mediterranean formula' (Selim 1997: 71). The Mediterranean forum was to be focused on non-political issues, but Egypt went further by indicating a willingness to consider the establishment of a Conference of Security and Cooperation for the Mediterranean (CSCM) inspired by the then Organization for Security and Cooperation in Europe. It was made clear that Iraq and Iran should have the opportunity to join eventually. In short, Egypt was willing to add a political-security dimension to the Euro-Mediterranean dialogue (Selim 1997: 73). This being said, the CSCM plan was eventually abandoned as being too ambitious, but the 'CSCM methodology' which consists of three levels, namely the political/security, the economic and socio-cultural level, was later to form the framework for the future Euro-Mediterranean agreement.

1. *European Negotiations.* Gillespie argues that Spain played a central part in the formulation and implementation of the Euro-Med Partnership framework. The reason behind Spain's increasingly influential role in the Mediterranean since the mid-1980s was its membership of the EU, domestic political stability and economic growth, the call for a comprehensive Mediterranean approach, improved relations with Morocco and Algeria, and the introduction of a more pragmatic policy towards Israel (Gillespie 1997: 37; Segal 1991: 261). France had always been the leading actor in relation to the shaping of Europe's Middle East and North African policies and Spain had been the junior partner. This had occasionally caused frictions between the two, for example over the role of the US in the EU's Mediterranean policies, but the main focus remained on cooperation. However, from Spain's perspective, relations with France were important in order to establish pro-Mediterranean alliances (a Mediterranean lobby) within the EC/EU with sufficient punch enabling the southern EU members to secure a balance between the EU's eastern and southern commitments (Gillespie 1997: 38).

The internal EU negotiations, which led to the launching of the Euro-Med Partnership took place primarily between 1994 and 1995. Gillespie identifies a 'pro-Mediterranean lobby' within the EU consisting of France and Spain as the leading characters and Portugal and Italy as the supporting acts (Gillespie 1991: 39). It was this constellation which was the driving force in the negotiations. The drafts to the Barcelona declaration were to some extent based on the 1991 Spanish-Morocco Friendship Treaty and, in order to secure the consent of the non-member states, a study of their previous agreements with the Community. In order to move forward, however, the key obstacle was to overcome the objections of the northern member states, most notably Germany, the UK and the Netherlands, whose primary interests were focused on relations with Eastern Europe and the EU's future enlargement in that region. Spain supported the European opening to the East, but it was Spanish Prime Minister González who leaned on Germany and threatened to block the eastern enlargement, unless the EU accepted the importance of the Mediterranean (Gillespie 1991: 39).

In 1994, at the summit in Essen, Germany came round to 'accept the notion that the southern frontier was crucial to the Union's stability and that there was a need to rebalance EU's external relations. With the Germans on board, resistance from other countries declined early in 1995' (Gillespie 1991: 39). In 1995, at the Cannes summit the proposal for the Euro-Med Partnership was approved with a budget of 4.7 billion ECU (Hollis 1997: 23). With this decision the scene was set for the Barcelona Conference in 1995.

2. *Redefining European Security.* During the Cold War, the Mediterranean Sea had a double role from a security perspective, on the one hand delineating Europe's frontier to the South, and on the other being the secondary frontier in the East–West Cold War rivalry. To the East, Europe's frontier was the Iron Curtain, but as it disappeared, the Mediterranean Sea remained a clear definition of the border between North and South (Fenech 1997: 150). Eastern Europe became an 'internal' security issue, whereas the Mediterranean at first was regarded as an external security issue of lesser importance. In short, in Europe the end of the Cold War sparked a debate over how to conceptualize and redefine the concept of security. It also stressed that the need to identify the organization/framework was best equipped to facilitate the task of providing collective security for Europe as a whole, but just as much in the Mediterranean. On the Mediterranean security agenda were issues such as Lebanon, Israel and the Palestinians, Israel and her Arab neighbours, the civil war in Algeria, proliferation of weapons of mass destruction, drugs trafficking and, as said, the absence of socio-economic development and political stability (Blank 2000: 25). The problem was that the Mediterranean, which emerged as the favoured post-Cold War notion for the area, had never been—and will never be—a unitary term. In the light of this, some argued that it would be futile to attempt to devise a single approach to the Mediterranean, instead 'allied interventions throughout the area must now be rationalized on a case-by-case basis' (Blank 2000: 28-29).

When discussing the security dimension of Europe's relations to the Middle East and the Mediterranean, the role of the USA is vital for the full picture. This transatlantic relationship will be dealt with later, but from a US perspective, the Mediterranean is not a coherent geo-strategic space, nor has there been a bureaucratic or academic tradition to regard the area as one (Lesser 1999: 212-13). This has complicated the US approach to the issues facing the Mediterranean.

A brief *tour d'horizon* will show that the three security organizations during the early 1990s sought to improve bilateral relations to the Mediterranean and Middle Eastern countries, not within a common framework for a collective security arrangement, but rather on a bilateral and Euro-centric basis (Fenech 1997: 150). The potential main contenders to the challenge of devising a security arrangement for the area were NATO, the WEU and the OSCE. It was only after the security organizations had begun to address the issue of central European security issues that the Mediterranean gained prominence.

NATO remained focused on the challenges related to the changes in East and Central Europe and the increasing levels of violence in Yugoslavia. Although NATO launched a 'Mediterranean Initiative' in 1995, 'most analysts agree that the Mediterranean does not present Europe with any military threats' (Spencer 1999: 204). At first, the role of the WEU was uncertain in relation to NATO. Nevertheless, it was involved in a dialogue with most of the southern Mediterranean states, yet it remained the junior organization compared to NATO. In the long term, it appeared that 'the WEU could become a suitable instrument to co-ordinate Europe's security concerns with those of the Mediterranean neighbours' as the potential instrument of a EU Common Foreign and Security Policy (Fenech 1997: 173). The OSCE is a collective security forum and not an alliance, which differentiates it from the other two organizations. The OSCE has a Mediterranean dialogue and has granted observer status to Morocco, Tunisia, Algeria, Egypt and Israel. The main problem is the 'OSCE's difficulty to translate theory into practice [which] may represent a measure of how distant the prospect of integrating the Mediterranean region with Europe remains' (Fenech 1997: 173).

Although the direct military threats to Europe may be limited, the proliferation of weapons of mass destruction and the stalemated peace process are cases for concern, though the risk of a spillover or direct attack on Europe is debatable as the attack on the USA with, for example, anthrax-infected letters in October 2001 showed. These risks, however, which could affect Europe are the non-military challenges stemming from an uneven socio-economic development and the social and political imbalance of the Middle Eastern states (Spencer 1999: 204).

The European Union and the Middle East from the 1995 Barcelona Conference until 2000

The purpose of this section is first to outline the nature of the European Union's Mediterranean Partnership initiative, which was launched in Barcelona in November 1995, and, secondly, to discuss the EU's role in the Middle East peace process. The third step will be to focus on the status of the relationship with the GCC. The chapter will conclude with a note on relations with Iraq, which have been complicated by the internal as well as transatlantic disagreements.

The Euro-Mediterranean Partnership: Barcelona 1995

The most central event in the European Union's relations to the Middle East and North Africa has been the Euro-Med Partnership initiative, which was launched at a conference in November 1995 in Barcelona. Besides the EU member states and institutions, the Palestinian Authority, Algeria, Cyprus, Egypt, Israel, Jordan, Lebanon, Malta, Morocco, Syria, Tunisia and Turkey participated, also the Arab Maghreb Union, the Arab League and Mauritania were in attendance as observers. Because of the UN Security Council Resolution 731 relating to the Lockerbie bombing, Libya was not invited. The USA and Russia did not participate either, as it was a clear attempt by the EU to enhance its profile as an international actor in its own right.

At the conference two documents were approved. 'The Barcelona Declaration' marked a new approach by the EU towards the Mediterranean and the Middle East. The agreement was aimed at creating a common, multilateral approach to the relations, and establishing a 'partnership', that is, the Euro-Mediterranean Partnership. Three sections were laid down in the Declaration—political and security, economic and financial, and, finally, the socio-cultural sections.

First, there was a political and security dimension, the aim of which was to establish 'a common area of peace and stability'. The signatories of the Declaration agreed that they would

> act in accordance with the United Nations Charter and the Universal Declaration of Human Rights, as well as other obligations under international law...develop the rule of law and democracy in their countries...respect human rights and fundamental freedoms and guarantee the effective legitimate exercises of such rights and freedoms (The Barcelona Declaration, European Parliament 1999a: 210) .

Secondly, the aim of an 'economic and financial partnership' was to create an area of shared prosperity. The way of achieving this was by financial and economic cooperation and, most importantly, by establishing a free trade area by 2010 which 'will cover most trade with due observance of the obligations resulting from the WTO'. The free trade was also to include agriculture, although the Declaration did not fail to mention that this was only 'as far as the various agricultural policies allow'—a veiled reference to the protectionist dimension of the Common Agricultural Policy of the EU. The intention was to conclude association agreements with each of the Mediterranean partners and formulate national indicative programmes for financial assistance where the EU then would support the economic transition process. The next step would then be to encourage integration between the southern Mediterranean states, which, if successful, would ultimately result in a single market more or less similar to the existing version within the EU (Joffé 1997: 16).

Thirdly, a partnership in social, cultural and human affairs aimed at 'developing human resources, promoting understanding between cultures and exchanges between civil societies'. The signatories agreed to 'strengthen their co-operation to reduce migratory pressures, among other things through vocational training programmes and programmes of assistance for job creation'. Also social development and the health sector was emphasized as areas of particular importance for sustainable development (The Barcelona Declaration, European Parliament 1999a: 214-15).

The second document adopted at Barcelona was the 'Work Programme' and the aim of it was 'to implement the objectives of the Barcelona Declaration, and to respect its principles, through regional and multilateral actions'. In other words, the 'Work Programme' identified the actions to be taken in relation to the aims of the Declaration and gave recommendations on which level the meetings were to be held (The Work Programme, European Parliament 1999a: 214-15). The Barcelona Declaration and the Work Programme formed the starting point for a process—the 'Barcelona Process'. It is important to be aware of the fact that after 1995 there were two processes in motion: the Middle East peace process/the Madrid peace process, which was sponsored by the USA, and the EU's Barcelona Process. Officially, the Barcelona process was to be seen as a distinct, but complementary process to the Madrid process. However, maintaining a clear distinction soon proved impossible since the state of the Madrid process influenced the Barcelona process.

In the aftermath of the Barcelona Conference, it was argued that the uniting factor for all around the Mediterranean was fear (*The Economist* 1995: 39). From a Middle East and North African perspective it was, as previously mentioned, the fear of a revitalized 'Fortress Europe', which would ignore the plight of the region and expel immigrants, further undermining the prospects for the region. From a European perspective, it was fear of migration and of Islamic fundamentalism and 'tacit admission that the Mediterranean had become a security problem' (Tovias 1996: 39). The fear bounded in the political and social instability, which ultimately could affect European security. Three main factors contributed to the situation. The demographic explosion in the region, and the 'slow economic growth and high unemployment rates' as well as 'the political vacuum arising from the inability of Arab regimes to broaden their bases by creating the consensus which would legitimise their regimes and integrate political Islam within national political systems' (Aliboni 1996: 30). The European fear of migration stemmed from the difficulties and failures experienced with regard to the integration of Muslim immigrants. Furthermore, the European countries, at least for the time being, have little wish to become 'melting pots' and generally appear deeply reluctant to become multicultural societies. Thus, the EU's ambition with the Euro-Med Partnership was to support and speed up the economic development and democratization of economic and political institutions in the region, which ideally would result in political stabilization.

Was the Euro-Med Partnership a step in the right direction? The dilemma was (and is) to ensure that the added economic inflow from the EU is supplemented by political reform. The latter has been hard to achieve since the repressive governments of the region have proved their durability and their immunity to sudden changes. This is also why *The Economist* (1995) described the political and security dimension of the Barcelona Declaration as 'waffle'. Democracy and human rights in the Middle East in general will be given more attention in Chapter 7, but the Arab world remains extremely sensitive of Western/European projects being forced upon them. The ironic aspect of this imposition of 'Euro-thinking' is that the introduction of democracy in the area could lead to Islamists gaining power through a popular election, which would be in direct opposition to EU interests (Niblock 1998: 5).

Democratization of the Arab world may be pressed for by the EU, but will be fruitless unless sought by the Arabs themselves. As a first step the EU can support the strengthening of the civil societies, since 'the strengthening of the civil society in the Arab world is the only way to support a process of democratisation predicated on both the facts and the values of the indigenous cultures' (Aliboni 1996: 31). Having said this, the prevailing view seems to be that there will be no substantial progress until a viable solution has been found to the Arab–Israeli conflict, and this will be the case with all three aspects of the Euro-Med Partnership (Joffé 1997: 21). As regards the economic dimension of the Euro-Med Partnership, the Mediterranean states are bound to resist demands for transparency when it comes to an economic restructuring, since it would undermine the patronage system operated by the state elite. Nevertheless, since 1995 Turkey, Morocco, Israel, Jordan, Syria and Tunisia have signed various types of agreements with the EU (Parfitt 1997: 873; Young 1998: 30).

Still, it remains to be seen what the effects of the free trade agreements may be on the area and the individual states. Most industries in the Mediterranean have been dominated by the public sector, and with their present level of competitiveness they will be unable to survive the international competition from the EU. The closure and/or restructuring of companies will inevitably lead to increased levels of unemployment, which will contradict one of the central aims of the Euro-Med Partnership, namely job creation. In addition to this, free trade principles are to be viewed with some scepticism, since one of the objectives of the EU is to limit the movement of people across borders. Moreover, it seems certain that the EU will hinder any introduction of free trade in the agricultural sector at least for the time being, though much may change with a reform of the Common Agricultural Policy (CAP).

Lastly, in relation to the cultural and social dimension of the Partnership, the barriers to progress are also here related to the absence of any solution of the political conflicts tormenting the area. Essentially, the flow and exchange of information, via the Internet, through NGO networks, the media, and so on, is to a very large extent impossible to control. It is likely that it will thus be countered with resistance by the Mediterranean governments, since the information could lead to opposition and criticism of the regimes and eventual dissidence (Joffé 1997: 27).

The European Union and the Madrid Peace Process after 1995

1. *Syria and Israel.* After the conclusion of the Oslo II agreement in 1995, the next event in the peace process was the Syrian–Israeli negotiations at the Wye Plantation in the USA, in December 1995 and January 1996. The talks concentrated on the return of the Golan Heights to Syria, security and, more generally, the normalization of the relationship between the two countries. In January 1996, however, the bilateral talks were suspended and the election in May of the Likud government, led by Benjamin Netanyahu, soon complicated relations with Syria and the Arab world even further.

Lebanon has always been in a particularly vulnerable position in the peace process with Israel's unilaterally declared 'security-zone' in the southern part of the country and Syria's *de facto* control of other parts of the country. Israel's operation, Grapes of Wrath, conducted in April 1996 was an unsuccessful attempt to eliminate the violent opposition of terrorism from the Islamist groups, Hamas and Hizbollah, operating in Lebanon. The US led the mediations that resulted in a cessation of hostilities and a document of understanding between Israel, Syria and Lebanon. From Syria's perspective, the control of Lebanon has been the major—and perhaps final—bargaining chip for Syria in its strife to regain the Golan Heights through negotiations. Therefore, when Israel proposed a withdrawal from Lebanon as a condition for a peace deal with Lebanon, it was rejected by Beirut because of pressure from Damascus, who controlled the political situation in Lebanon. For Israel, the optimal solution was to separate negotiations with Lebanon from negotiations with Syria.

Besides expressing its support for peace negotiations, the EU had no influence on the negotiations and meditations between Israel, Syria and Lebanon during 1996. Nevertheless, in February 1996, the EU Troika, led by Italy, did visit Syria where, among other things, it expressed the EU's intention to appoint a special envoy to the region who would enhance the EU's role in negotiations. At least in a Middle East context, the concept of a special envoy made sense, given the limitations of the Troika's involvement. Not only was the length of any visit by the Troika to any country limited, but also the lack of continuity affected the chances of obtaining results. A special envoy would to some extent make up the shortcomings of the situation.

In November 1996, the Council appointed the Spanish ambassador Miguel Angel Moratinos as the special envoy to the Middle East. The mandate of the special envoy was defined broadly, but was essentially to report to the EU institutions of the developments in the peace process, establish and maintain relations between the EU and the relevant actors involved, and ensure that EU—and EU member states— policies and initiatives were well coordinated. It is also to ensure 'complementarity' between the Union and the US in the efforts to push forward the peace process (Guttman 1998–99: 30-31). As the negotiations surrounding the Oslo Accords testify, some negotiations are often conducted via back channels, which as a method of negotiation must be next to impossible for an organization like the EU to establish. As said before, the lack of secrecy and the fear of leaks undermined the EU's credibility, especially in a hyper-sensitive environment like the Middle East. Although Moratinos apparently was able to ensure a degree of secrecy, the nature of the EU organizations inevitably reflect on him and his position. This enhanced the position of Moratinos's American counterpart, Dennis Ross.

2. The Palestinian Elections 1996. After the establishment of the Palestinian National Authority (PNA) and the withdrawal of Israeli troops from several West Bank towns and Gaza in January 1996, the Palestinians elected a 'President' and members to a Legislative Council. Yasser Arafat stood unopposed. Israel remained in control over foreign policy, the currency, external security, immigration and settlements, but the Legislative Council was granted powers to legislate on issues such as education and health, local government, economic affairs and so on (European Parliament 1999a: 37). At this point, the use of the word 'Palestine' deserves a mention. Palestine was of course the name for the area pre-1948. Since the mid-1990s it has been used, formally and informally, to refer to the new Palestinian entity, that is, the West Bank and Gaza and East Jerusalem, which are now in parts under the control of the Palestinians and which in time will form the basis of a Palestinian state.[2] The EU's political and financial contribution to the holding of elections was quite significant. Some 17 million ECU were donated via the CFSP; 7 million ECU were earmarked for the preparation of the technical aspects of the election, such as the establishment of polling stations and a press centre, and 10 million ECU were spent

---

2.   Historically, the name Palestine was given to Judaea and Samaria by emperor Hadrian, who wanted to eliminate the historical ties of the Jews to Judaea, in the year 132 AD.

on ensuring international monitoring of the elections. At the end of the day, the EU coordinator concluded that the elections had been 'reasonably free', in spite of minor irregularities. The Troika, a delegation from the European Parliament and Commission Vice-president Marin visited the West Bank and Gaza in relation to the election (European Commission 1999a: 38).

3. *Israel and the Palestinians.* The Likud and its leader Mr Netanyahu won Israel's General Election in May 1996. The Likud party was committed to the ideological concept of a 'Greater Israel', which complicated justification for any territorial concessions made to the Palestinians. Moreover, the Likud victory came in the wake of Hamas attacks, which had strengthened the political discourse and public demands for 'security'. The Likud government managed to bring the peace process to ruins during its tenure. About the only progress made was the Hebron Protocol, which was signed on 17 January 1997, by the Israeli government and the PNA and provided for the redeployment of Israeli troops from parts of Hebron and a timetable for redeployments from other West Bank cities. In relation to the Hebron Protocol, letters of assurance were sent from the US Secretary of State to Israel and to the Palestinians. Also, the EU was encouraged by the US to send a letter of assurance to the Palestinians wherein the EU stated that it would use all its political influence to ensure that the agreements were implemented in full (Jensen and Laursen 2000: 55-56).

As one of the concerns of the Likud government was security, this led to ever increasing demands that the Palestinians countered terrorism in the territories controlled by the PNA. Between April 1997 and October 1998 the EU enhanced its relations and assistance to the PNA, especially in security related areas. Cooperation between the EU and representatives of Palestinian security forces was agreed to, and the EU has financed the education and training of police forces and administrative units as well as providing some equipment (European Parliament 1999a: 45). In order to improve relations between Israel and the EU and to eliminate some of the barriers to Palestinian development, the EU established an EU–Israeli Joint Dialogue, which has established working groups on expert level that meet regularly. The main results have been to ensure some pragmatic improvements in the access for Palestinian workers and businessmen to Israel, as well as improving the procedures, and access for Palestinian cargo and trade in and out of

Israel. Another important aspect of the dialogue has been simply to facilitate dialogue and confidence-building measures at all levels between Israelis and Palestinians. This was, for example, the case with regard to the Euro-Mediterranean Conference in Malta in 1997 where Arafat and Foreign Minister Levy met, and the visit to the European Parliament by a joint Israeli-Palestinian delegation of politicians (European Parliament 1999a: 46).

Once More: Wye?

After more than twelve months of inertia in the peace process it was the EU under the UK presidency and special envoy Moratinos, who eventually managed to persuade Israel and the Palestinians to resume negotiations over a second redeployment from the West Bank. However, the EU was not alone as the negotiations in London on 4–5 May 1998 took place in the presence of US Secretary of State Albright. As with the Hebron redeployment, the central issues were the percentage of land from which Israel should withdraw, security, the safe passage between Gaza and the West Bank and the opening of Gaza airport. Israel also demanded that the clauses in the Palestinian National Charter that called for the destruction of the state of Israel were abrogated. The Wye Memorandum was signed in Washington DC on 23 October 1998. With regards to the West Bank, the PNA would be in full control of 18.2% (Area A), partial control of 21.8% (Area B) and Area C would be 60%. Furthermore, two safe passages were agreed to, and the plans for the Gaza Airport were approved.[3] Surprisingly, the CIA was to monitor the implementation of the Palestinian security plans as a guarantee for Israel (Jensen and Laursen 2000: 56-58).

The Wye Memorandum was 'short lived'. Between October and December 1998, Israel reluctantly undertook one partial redeployment and authorized the opening of the Gaza Airport. US President Clinton visited Gaza and witnessed the voting of the National Council on the abrogation of the offensive clauses in the National Charter, which had been a part of the Wye Memorandum. The EU had not been invited to join the Wye negotiations, although special envoy Moratinos was in the USA and was being constantly updated (Guttman 1998–99: 30-31). After the signing of the Memorandum, President Arafat stopped over in Europe to thank the EU for its support and financial assistance and

3. http://www.state.gov/www/regions/nea

called for the continued support of the EU to implement the new agreement, which he duly received (European Parliament 1999a: 47). Mr Netanyahu flew straight home.

In December 1998 the process reached a complete deadlock when Israel's government suspended any further implementation of the Memorandum. During the Autumn Israel had intensified the demands for the Palestinian leadership to end the incitement to violence and stop calling for the release of Palestinians who had killed Israelis. However, but most importantly perhaps, was the question of Palestinian statehood. PNA President Arafat had on several occasions declared that he would proclaim a Palestinian state on 4 May 1999 at the end of the interim period (that is, five years after the Oslo Agreement) if no progress had been made. Arafat's threats must be seen as a primarily tactical response to the situation, since it was widely held that a Palestinian state at that time would be unfeasible. One reason was simply because of the lack of geographical cohesiveness of the Palestinian entity. Another was that the Israeli government made it very clear that a unilateral decision to declare statehood would not be looked favourably upon, and it would most likely lead to violence and a formal annexation of the Occupied Territories. The EU and the US eventually managed to convince Arafat to postpone the declaration. At the Berlin Summit in March 1999, the EU expressed its support for the Palestinians and signalled its preparedness to recognize a future Palestinian state created ideally based on negotiations, but otherwise unilaterally declared (European Parliament 1999a: 48-49).

In Israel, the suspension of the Wye Memorandum by the Netanyahu government led to a vote of no confidence, which resulted in general and prime ministerial elections on 17 May 1999. The new Labour government led by Ehud Barak was elected on an agenda which promised the resumption of the peace process, and a withdrawal from Lebanon on the basis of UN SCR 425. To the surprise of some, by June 2000, Israel had withdrawn completely from Lebanon. Although the negotiations with Syria were resumed occasionally there was no early breakthrough. Furthermore, with the death of Syrian President Hafiz al-Asad, and the succession of his son Bashar to the presidency, any peace moves vis-à-vis Israel could not be expected before Bashar al-Asad's power position within Syria is consolidated.

In July 2000, President Clinton convened a summit at Camp David which was attended by Prime Minister Barak, and Palestinian Authority President, Yasser Arafat. In spite of two weeks of talks, the summit ended without any deal. In spite of the lack of visible results, it is important to note that core issues such as Jerusalem, the refugees and the question of Palestinian statehood were actually debated in an official setting.[4]

Assistance to the Palestinians: The View from Europe
In 1998, the EU reviewed the effects of its political and economic assistance to the Palestinians and the peace process. Clearly, the EU's political willingness to assist the Palestinians economically had been successful. As previously discussed, the number of partners with whom Israel can negotiate in the peace process are limited, and the EU's efforts as a player in the process had been in securing the continued coherence of the Palestinians as a partner for Israel. Having said this, the economic assistance had not yielded any notable progress in relation to economic cooperation. This was, on the one hand, blamed on Israel's closures of the West Bank and Gaza, which immediately put the Palestinian economy in reverse; on the other hand, it was blamed on the Palestinian Authority's management of resources. Therefore, in 1998 at a post-Wye Donors' Conference in Washington the EU pledged to donate 400 million ECU over a period of five years, but it was later made clear that the funds were to be allocated primarily to development projects, and not to the budget of the Palestinian Authority. Together with Norway, the EU co-chaired the Ad Hoc Liaison Committee, a follow-up from the Conference and coordinates international assistance to the Palestinians. This position also provided the EU with a further opportunity to influence the process.

The European Union and the Gulf Cooperation Council
As mentioned above, 1995 was regarded as a turning point when the focus was shifted towards a strengthening of the political dialogue and, especially, economic cooperation. It was understandable since economic and energy interdependence are the key ingredients of the relationship and what have brought the two together (Saleh 1999: 15). There have been a few advances in areas related to economic cooperation: decentralized business relations, management training, university co-

---

4.   Cf. the Middle East summit at Camp David homepage: http://www.state.gov/www/regions/nga

operation. Some of the central aims of cooperation were to strengthen transnational business activities by arranging meetings and conferences for different business sectors, establishing funds earmarked to support business initiatives, establishing networks and by giving technical advice.

Cultural cooperation was also promoted in order to further understanding between the civil societies, and it has primarily been aimed at parliaments, NGOs and the media, to mention but a few examples. The cultural cooperation is also an attempt to reduce the tensions related to issues such as human rights where the definitions of terms differ considerably between the Europe and the Gulf. This has caused rows, especially between the European Parliament and Gulf states such as the UAE (Saleh 1999: 15). A senior EU official explained to the authors that discussing human rights with the Gulf states was a complicated and often fruitless exercise and the subject had previously led to walkouts from meetings. However, in recent years there has been a slow change in attitude, which means that the subject is now possible to discuss, even though the most concrete accomplishments appear to be lengthy communiqués. From a European perspective, progress on the issue is also heavily dependent on the interests and priorities of the EU presidency where ignorance or lack of interests from the political side may jeopardize previous achievements and let the issue slip into the background.

The Case of Iraq
After more than six years of different types of international sanctions and sporadic military attacks, it is evident that the US 'dual containment' policies have failed, as has the Union's policy of selective accommodation with Iraq. Saddam Hussein has remained in power— and by 2001 it is generally accepted that the main recipient of the sanctions and military attacks has thus been the Iraqi people, and not its leadership (Darwish 2000: 13-14; Baram 2000: 194; Serfaty 1998: 7). In the aftermath of the Second Gulf War, the UN humanitarian intervention in Kurdistan, 'Operation Safe Havens', was at first a success. However, as the media spotlight shifted away from the plight of the Kurds in Northern Iraq, the Western governments disengaged by handing over the task to the UN without contributing sufficient resources to run the operations on a satisfactory basis. Having said this, the intervening Western governments have so far upheld the 'no-fly-zone' in

Northern Iraq in protection of the Kurds, even though it is causing increasing tensions between the Western allies (Wheeler 1997: 404). France has chosen to dissociate itself from the US air strikes in Northern Iraq since January 1997, and criticized the US handling of the crisis regarding the weapons inspectors in 1997–98. In order to be the leading motor in foreign policy France seeks to maintain a leverage over Germany, but remains unable to influence the UK, the key ally of the USA. In relation to Iraq and the Gulf in general, Serfaty raises the point that with its close ties to the USA and its increasing influence in Europe, the UK may be the 'credible broker' between the USA and the Union, but also within the Union. In other words the UK would be able to balance the US position with the French demands and German passiveness. The idea will be elaborated on in the following chapter and related to the issue of the future of transatlantic relations and interests vis-à-vis the Middle East in general (Serfaty 1998: 7). With regard to Iraq, however, the initiatives of the Western part of the international community, including the EU, may have alleviated some short-term problems, but it has been incapable and/or unwilling to address the long-term problems facing the country. The USA and the EU have also been unable to establish a common ground and define a shared policy towards Iraq and the Gulf.

6 |

Reflections on the State of European Union Policies towards the Middle East by 2001

The purpose of this chapter is to present a series of concluding reflections on the status of the policies of the European Union towards the Middle East as of 2001.

The Euro-Mediterranean Partnership

As previously mentioned, one of the central purposes of the Euro-Med Partnership is to limit the flow of immigrants from the Middle East and from North Africa. In order to achieve this, the EU encourages and supports economic development on the shores of the southern Mediterranean through financial and technical assistance.

As the southern Mediterranean sees development and job creation on its shores, the chance of achieving prosperity and thus stability in the region will increase. The hoped-for result is that the interest in migration to Europe would decrease. However, socio-economic development initiatives are nearly always time-consuming processes, and the problem with the Euro-Med Partnership is that its long-term focus on development addresses a real and present problem with a strategy which may, or indeed may not, bear fruit only in the long term. Adding to this, signs of an economic recession are beginning to show in 2001.

In addition, there are other issues that limit the possibilities of curbing migration. One example is the issue of wage remittances (the money/wages that expatriates send home). Wage remittances constitute a key component of the domestic economies of the Partnership states, and the amount is frequently higher than the actual amount of foreign direct investment attracted to the countries in the region (White 1999: 3). Therefore, any serious attempts to control the borders would most likely have repercussions on the domestic economies, which in turn would have national security implications for the leaders of the

Partnership states. In other words, since too stringent control on migration to Europe could be politically dangerous, one must ask whether the Partnership states are not merely paying lip service to the EU's demands when accepting anti-immigration dimension of the Euro-Med Partnership. Also, a change in leadership in the Middle East could lead to a take-over by Islamic parties or groups, which would not be in the interest of the EU. Regardless, any hopes the EU might have to curb immigration immediately are questionable and would indeed only be possible seen in a very long-term perspective.

Another issue related to migration to Europe is the wish to escape violent conflicts, as has been the case with, for example, the Palestinians, the Iraqis and more recently the Algerians. Additionally, one of the reasons for Spain's dominant role in the shaping of the EU's Mediterranean policies during the 1990s was because of the Algerian civil war, which limited France's ability to manoeuvre as a former colonial power in the region.

There are also factors in Europe, which have to be taken into account when discussing the issue of migration. The demand for cheap labour in Europe also fuels migration. According to White 'there is a profound demand for legal, and increasingly, illegal immigrant labour in Europe' (White 1999: 3). Other factors stem from the obvious disparities in levels of income, which stimulates further the interest in Europe as an immigrant destination. This is amplified by the southern Mediterranean's access to the European entertainment industry and media, which usually provide a somewhat distorted and rather glossy picture of Europe.

Clearly, the neo-liberal policies of the EU, and other international financial organizations are not enough to assist the economic development in the Mediterranean region. Instead of listing needed reforms in the southern Mediterranean, it is possible to identify areas where reforms within the EU itself would both benefit the EU, as well as enhance the chances of economic development in the Mediterranean— again, in the long-term.

The EU managed to reform the Common Agricultural Policy (CAP) in 1999. The CAP, in brief, is a subsidy of the Union's agricultural production and exports, and a protection from external competition. The EU, challenged only by the US, is one of the leading players in the world agricultural market. From a Mediterranean perspective, agricultural export produce, for example, olive oil, tomatoes and wine, have been barred from entering the European market since the mid-1980s, essentially to limit the external competition to Spain's agricultural sector after its accession in 1986 (White 1999: 8). As a result of this, export to Europe has become next to impossible, and many rural areas have become increasingly unable to provide a livelihood for the local population, which has resulted in a steady migration to urban areas and abroad. In addition to this, unfavourable climatic conditions, bad regional planning (or lack of the same) and national politics have not helped. It is still too early to evaluate the consequences of the reformed CAP. But the spin-off is most likely to increase the chances of further sustainable development of the Mediterranean agricultural sector, and this will result in a demand for labour in the Mediterranean rural areas—and not in Europe.

Another issue of importance for the Euro-Med Partnership is the definition of Europe's identity, which needs reconsideration. In the post-Communist era, international organizations of which the EU member states were members, as well as the EU, identified Europe by an often simplified 'us' and 'them' approach. There was a perceived need to define a new enemy, which would delineate Europe's borders, and unite in the uncertain post-Cold War period. There was a tendency towards considering fundamentalist Muslim regimes and organizations as a new enemy—a process that the terrorist actions of 11 September 2001 onwards has strengthened. This was reflected, for example, in relation to issues such as visas, and potential membership applicants, which also goes some way in explaining Turkey's strained relationship with the EU. White argues that

> Europe, if it really pursues a relationship that goes further than being a trade partner, has to free itself from the obsessive search of new enemies, from a fortress mentality...European officials and its citizenry must challenge such efforts, not only because they defy reality, but because of their inherent destructiveness (White 1999: 9).

Arab officials[1] regard the present peace process between Israel and the Arab world as a way of finding a way to absolve the sins of the past. A comprehensive peace settlement would presumably lead to changes within the Arab world, both in the political environment and the societies, but it could also lead to improved relations with Europe, and a new kind of openness. Ambitious as it may sound, the Arab world

1. In conversations with the authors.

may be revitalized as a potential trading partner and political ally of Europe. Therefore Europe needs to revise its perception and understanding of the Middle East.

Democracy and Human Rights

Democratization and human rights are frequently emerging and sensitive questions in the relationship between the EU and the Middle East. Due to the polarization of the Cold War, the interests of the 'Western' part of the international community have granted support to regimes, which often had a pro-Western outlook, while paying scant attention to their human rights record and to their degree of democratization. It comes as no surprise that, from a Middle Eastern perspective, there has always been a cultural sensitivity to externally imposed schemes and projects.

The importance of the EU's advocacy of the ideals of democratization in international relations is generally acknowledged, and the Union's stance on democratization has indeed improved the awareness of a need for an opening of the political systems in the Middle East. Yet, according to Tim Niblock, the policies of democracy and economic liberalization, the basic strategy of the Partnership, are 'mutually antagonistic' because economic liberalization frequently creates social tensions, and control of social upheavals may be more easily handled by a non-democratic government (Niblock 1998: 5). However, 'the practical framework for its interaction with the policies of the Middle East (and perhaps other developing countries) needs to be such that they can bring real benefits to the peoples of the region' (Niblock 1998: 6). In spite of its conceptualizing problems, Niblock argues that a 'good governance' approach is a way in which the EU can involve itself in the region.

As has been discussed earlier, political declarations on democracy coming from the Middle East are often without much substance. Instead, the way forward would be to establish a mutual framework on the concept of 'good governance', which would include the establishment of cooperation, links, and other exchanges between policy-makers and academics. There is also a need for the EU to produce a more nuanced approach to democratizations taking into account the regional specifics. But this is by no means going to be understood as an advocacy of turning a blind eye to human rights violations and so forth.

One dimension of the democratization debate is 'the structural relationship between state and society' (Niblock 1998: 2). Essentially, the state controls the social groupings through a patron–client relationship. The main interest of the elitist groups is to maintain the *status quo* of the regime, and to ensure the regime will quell radical opposition, which may endanger their own positions. This means that elitist groups within the state could very well oppose any moves towards political liberalization, as it would endanger their own position. This is also an important aspect in relation to the issue of the changing leaderships in the region. Admittedly, with the clarity of hindsight, one could argue that the transition processes in Jordan and Syria were bound to go smoothly. Jordan, for one, has previously witnessed two peaceful transfers of power, which has not been the case with Syria. Nevertheless, both countries had a leading class who perceived the stability of the country—and their hold on power—to be more important than democracy. It appears that it is only after the new leaders have established their new power bases that the countries begin to witness political change. Having said this, the situation could naturally have turned out much differently had an alternative candidate with a sufficient backing appeared on the scene during the process.

One possible outcome of the political democratization in the Middle East is often overlooked in the European debate. Should some degree of democratization be implemented in the Middle East, the chance of an Islamist opposition winning the ballot—as it did in Algeria—is possible and will have to be taken into consideration when discussing issues like democratization.

In sum, according to Niblock, the international community, including the EU, should change its focus from liberal democracy to the concept of 'good governance', because it has a greater chance of changing the situation for the peoples of the region. The EU should then be seeking to promote 'stability based on popular acceptance' (Niblock 1998: 7).

When it comes to human rights, the Association Agreements, which have been signed as a part of the Euro-Med Partnership, contain human rights provisions and commitments to respect the rule of law. However, activist groups in Brussels argue that the EU perceives human rights as a 'side issue', and that the EU chooses instead to focus primarily on the economic dimensions of the relationship. To mention but a few examples, Israel allows 'mild physical pressure', Egypt is conducting an intense crackdown on the Islamist opposition, and Syria and Iraq are the *bêtes noires* on all counts. Still, Morocco is singled out as a country where modest degrees of improvements have been witnessed, and there could be hope that the trend is maintained (George 1998b: 12). According to George, this view is countered by the Commission, which argues that the fact that the human rights provisions have been included is a step in the right direction, and that the EU now has a legal obligation to take action if human rights are abused. If one was to take this at face value, there will quite possibly be sufficient evidence to suspend the Euro-Med Partnership indefinitely. Still, the Commission also argues that it would be unrealistic to expect a sea change in the Mediterranean Partnership states (George 1998b: 12).

Peace Process: After the Camp David Talks

The intention here is to discuss the situation in the aftermath of the Camp David talks, which took place in July 2000, and the recommendations of the Mitchell Report, and to outline future scenarios and discuss the future options for the EU in the process.

The talks were convened under US auspices, and led by a US president in his second and final term in office. For the first time, core issues, such as Jerusalem, refugees and Palestinian statehood were actually discussed in an official setting, which must be regarded as a positive step in the peace process. In spite of some apparent progress in the negotiations, the talks were eventually abandoned without any final settlement, which was what had been hoped for. It is clearly the US that has the political clout to act as a broker in the peace talks. The EU contributed with a proposal concerning the establishment of Jerusalem as an international city. The proposal was politely received, but treated as nothing more than yet another point to be considered.[2]

Two months after the breakdown of the Camp David negotiations, Ariel Sharon (then member of the Knesset, later Prime Minister) announced that he was going to visit the Temple Mountain in Jerusalem, a place sacred to Jews, Muslims and Christians alike. The visit on 28 September 2000 was considered as a provocation by the Palestinians, and was answered with a 'second intifada'. To stop the escalation

---

2. This attitude—to keep the EU out of the negotiations—was reflected several times during the negotiations, e.g. as the US president's spokesman, Joe Lockhart, was asked whether Clinton had had contacts with other world leaders and answered negatively (http://www.state.gov/www/regions/nea, press briefing, 5 July 2000).

of violence and its threat to the peace process, President Clinton met with representatives of the governments of Israel, Egypt, Jordan, of the Palestine Authority, of UN and EU at Sharm el-Sheikh in Egypt in October 2000. A concrete result of the Middle East Peace Summit was the decision to appoint a fact-finding commission, and to give it the task of proposing recommendations to end violence, to prevent its reoccurrence and to find a way back to the peace process (Mitchell Report, 2001).

The Sharm el-Sheikh Fact Finding Commission, which was soon to be named after its chairman, former US senator George Mitchell, included three other high-ranking persons; Javier Solana (EU High Representative), Suleyman Demirel (Turkish President) and the then Norwegian foreign minister, Thorbjørn Jagland. The result of its deliberations can be summarized in three points: end violence, rebuild confidence and resume negotiations (Mitchell Report, 2001).

The report was delivered on 30 April 2001 to the new US president George W. Bush, who at that time had taken no significant interest in Middle East affairs (or indeed in any other foreign affairs, unless they were seen as an obstacle to US freedom of action). After the terrorist acts of September 2001, the USA put pressure on especially Israel, that Israel and the Palestinian Authority should resume the peace process according to the outline of the Mitchell Report. By October Israel's Foreign Minister Simon Peres, was allowed by Ariel Sharon to meet again with Arafat after a longer break in the negotiations. To secure the coherence of the 'Coalition against Terrorism' the US put even further pressure on Israel by declaring its support for a Palestinian state, a wish also declared by British Prime Minister Blair, when meeting Arafat at 10 Downing Street, London in mid October 2001.

It should be possible to outline two future scenarios for the peace process. One scenario is that the US might at some point be able to persuade the two parties, Israel and the Palestinians, to negotiate a final settlement. Consequently, the declaration of Palestine would then be with the support of the USA and Israel. It is next to impossible to predict the specifics of any such deal, but whatever happens, one thing seems certain—it is *most* unlikely that it will favour the demands of the Palestinians. The USA, and the Clinton Administration in particular, has always been rather heavily biased in favour of Israel. The George W. Bush administration seemed at first to have adopted a slightly more even-handed approach to the Middle East, although this changed after a few months in office. The Administration has often criticized the Palestinian leadership's efforts to quell the violence in relation to the Al-Aqsa Intifada, and in spite of several visits to the White House by Ariel Sharon, inviting Arafat was not considered until October 2001. Moreover, there has been no significant efforts to restart any negotiations between the two sides before the terrorist attacks on Washington and New York, and the subsequent establishment of the coalition against terrorism has pressed President Bush to act. Regardless, the establishment of a Palestinian state will no doubt depend on external resources, aid and technical assistance *en masse*, and here the EU has ample room to operate.

Another scenario is that the US fails to secure a settlement between the two sides, and Yasser Arafat decides to declare a Palestinian state unilaterally. Any such move would indeed be very risky for the Palestinian leadership. As mentioned, Palestine is divided into cantons, separated by land controlled by Israel. If Arafat does declare statehood without Israel's consent, one response could be anything from studied neglect, bearing in mind the viability of a Palestinian state seems nearly nil without Israel's approval. Alternatively, it is quite possible that Israel, using a national security pretext, would decide to annex the West Bank and Gaza and eliminate any possibility of a Palestinian state in future. This, however, would not be a risk free approach for Israel, since such a move will not be without bloodshed, and the violence could ultimately trigger an intensely negative response from Arab states. The interesting question will be which line the US will take. Besides a few diplomatic victories in the Middle East, the USA policies have not been successful in the region. An escalation of violence in the wake of a declaration of statehood might lead the USA to reconsider its position and level of involvement in the peace process. Still the thought of the USA 'abandoning' the peace process would seem most unlikely. Rather, the question appears to be how far the USA will allow Israel to go in its response to the Palestinians. Another dimension could be whether any support of Israel could complicate US relations to the Gulf states and the access to oil, and how this could affect the US position.

If a final settlement is reached through US involvement, the European Union will have the opportunity to support and work within the framework of such an agreement. The 'payer versus player' concept is of use in the broader dimensions of the EU's role in the peace process. 'The payer' would be the organization which sponsors the agreements of the peace process financially, 'the player' would then be the actor which has sufficient power to broker, or at least participate in the shaping and establishment of political deals in the process. In the peace process, the European Union is 'a payer', since it has insufficient political power to broker political agreements—that is the task, of which only the US is capable. But it was the 'payer' who kept the peace process afloat making sure that the Palestinian Authority did not go bankrupt.

The EU is a 'player' and a 'payer' only when it operates within political frameworks, which nearly always have been defined by others, as for example in the case of the Oslo Accords/the Palestinians. A counter argument would be that the Union's financial support of the Palestinians has made it a 'player'. Even though the importance of the EU's relations with and support of the Palestinians must not be under-estimated, the larger political framework has, nonetheless, still been designed by others than the EU, although the EU has rarely been in opposition to the political agreements.

As an additional point, the appointment of a special envoy to the Middle East has enhanced the coordination of, and cooperation within the EU, but one could question whether the position will be of any special significance in the long term. The role of the special envoy, among other things, has been to focus on the actors in the peace process which were left out of the US-sponsored peace talks. For example, if Israel was negotiating with the Palestinians under US auspices, the special envoy would then be talking to the Syrians and the Lebanese. However, with Israel's withdrawal from Lebanon, at present the main focus is on the Palestinians, and secondarily on Syria and it is unthinkable that any of these would allow the EU to assume a leading position in the final peace talks. The special envoy's sphere of activity has thus decreased and limited the position to little more than a spokesperson and messenger for the EU. In sum, if a final settlement is agreed in future, it will fall to the EU to act within the boundaries of the established framework, and the EU's contribution in areas such as political relations and dialogue, confidence-building measures, and various types of assistance will surely be much appreciated.

In case of a unilateral declaration of independence, the EU would be faced with a serious dilemma, and it would ultimately have to decide whether supporting the Palestinians would be worth the trouble, and the political prize. The EU can choose to recognize Palestine and this will be in line with the EU's present policy. However, a unilaterally declared state is, as said, unlikely to have the support of the US. It is quite possible that the US would exert strong pressure on the EU in case the EU signals a willingness to recognize a unilaterally declared Palestinian state and the US–EU relations might suffer from these tensions. The chances are that the EU would argue that it indeed will recognize a state, but only if it is based on a negotiated settlement, thus favouring relations with Washington and leaving the Palestinians to their maker—and the Israelis. This, however, would seriously undermine the ambitions of the CFSP, and the EU's credibility in the Middle East, and beyond. One alternative source of support might be Russia, though the possible response will be a reluctance to recognize a state before it has proved its viability.

Russia

In the post-Cold War era, Russia has placed great stress on maintaining good relations with Washington, and nurturing its image as a credible international partner. This also means that Russia is less inclined to intervene diplomatically on behalf of the Palestinians, and in the Arab–Israeli conflict in general. A clear example of Russia going against Arab interests was the permission for a half million Jews to emigrate to Israel in the early part of the 1990s (Hermann 1994: 462-63). Consequently, without Russia as the principal—and only—advocate of Arab and Palestinian interests in the 'peace processes', the asymmetry of power becomes evident with the US controlling and shaping events in favour of Israel. Also, in the case of Iraq, Russia accepted US air raids on Baghdad, the capital of a former client state.

The Gulf Cooperation Council

The Euro–Arab dialogue faced trouble in 1979 because of the then EC's wish to exclude—or inability to include—political issues, especially such as the Palestinian question. The Arabs wanted the political dimension to be more at the core of the relationship, and since that was not to be the case, they broke off the dialogue. Later, with the establishment of the GCC, a new potential partner for the EU had emerged. However, because of political instability in the region, such as the Iran–Iraq War and the Soviet presence in Afghanistan, there was to be no progress until the 1988 armistice agreement between Iran and Iraq altered the political landscape in the Gulf. The 1988 EC–GCC Co-operation Agreement marked a change of approach to the region, and a willingness to include political issues on the agenda, such as the peace process and later the Second Gulf War. This approach was pursued further in the aftermath of the Cold War when the EU sought to fill a part of the power vacuum after Russia (Brandenburg 1994: 10-11). As the discussions in Chapter 5 showed, this trend survives today after the 1995 adjustment of the relationship, which is now shaped on the Euro-Med Partnership 'formula', that is, political dialogue, economic co-operation and cultural cooperation. The EU might wish in future to seek to integrate relations between the Mediterranean and the Gulf (Hollis 1997: 27). Still, the EU has accepted that the political dimension of the relationship, weak as it may be, is necessary in order to make advances in the fields of economic cooperation.

In general, the GCC states appear to be focused on revitalizing their economies by passing legislation and other measures in order to encourage foreign investment (Anonymous 2000: 3-4). The moves are urgently needed, because in spite of forecasts of economic growth, all is not well in the Gulf. The major challenge, or threat, is the demographic development.

> With an average of around 70 per cent of the region's indigenous popu-
> lation under the age of 30, population growth will continue to outstrip
> economic growth, pushing up employment rates among GCC nationals
> and depressing real per capita income growth' (Anonymous 2000: 3-4).

The GCC establishment of a customs union in November 1999 was a partial response to a demand from the Union before the EU would accept a free trade agreement. The deal had two implications. The aluminium and petrochemical industries gained improved access to the European markets, and the customs union has had the positive effect of strengthening the bargaining position of the GCC in relation to the on-going applications for World Trade Organization (WTO) membership (Anonymous 2000: 3-4). A positive assessment would thus be to say that the EU has gained from the deal, which has actually led the GCC states to a stronger bargaining position with an international organiza-tion, such as the WTO. The export/support of regional integration based on the EU's model is often perceived as a typical EU export to its external partners. For the EU, the GCC relations also mean that the GCC states, especially Saudi Arabia, can function as a mediator for the

EU. From the GCC perspective, the emphasis appears to have shifted from a desire to focus on the political dimensions of the relations, as during the Euro–Arab dialogue, to an increased focus on the economic aspects.

7 |

Conclusion

This chapter concentrates on three topics: the developments in EU's Middle East policies, the EU's actorness in the Middle East, and the future prospects for the EU's Middle East policies.

Changes in the EU's Relations with the Middle East

Relations with the Gulf States

As the Euro–Arab dialogue froze in the aftermath of Camp David 1978–79, the EC took an initiative to secure its top priority, namely access to the Arab energy resources. This was done through informal contacts with the Arab oil producers, but from 1981 by informal talks with the newly established Gulf Cooperation Council. Equally interesting is that the Gulf states were ready to enter into a close relationship with Europe at that time.

This must be seen as a result of the EC's generally pro-Arab attitude and the Venice Declaration in particular, as well as the Arab interests in European money and/or trade. At the beginning of 2000, the dialogue was focused on politics and economics, with the political dimension facilitating the smooth functioning of the economic dimension of the relations. A cultural dimension was also included, but has been of far less significance.

It must be stressed that human rights and democracy, at present, play a less significant role than anticipated by the EU, and especially by the EP. Furthermore, interviews conducted in Brussels in March 2000 by the authors revealed that these developments were of less concern to the European Commission. Moreover, the Arab side has voiced complaints that the Gulf dialogue had a seemingly low status for the EU. This was confirmed by a senior civil servant at the Council of Ministers, who essentially argued that 'it takes two to tango', and if the Arab side have no interests in maintaining the relations, there is not much the EU can do.

Peace Process

The EC's policies towards the Middle East peace process were shaped and defined roughly between 1973 and 1980, culminating with the Venice Declaration. The Declaration should be regarded as no more than a political signal, but it helped the EC to secure a good working relationship with the Arab world during the 1980s, especially during the first half of the 1980s when the New Cold War divided the world into the bipolar system.

The Venice Declaration became the point of reference for the EU when it chose to respond to developments in the peace process usually orchestrated by the USA and/or Israel, and which did not consider the interests of the Union's wishes. Moreover, the Declaration also marked the EU's attempt to profile itself as a 'third option' to the two super-powers, though this did not yield any particular results.

During the Cold War of the 1980s, the involvement of the EC was next to non-existent. The Madrid Process, which began in the aftermath of the Gulf War, saw the EU as only an observer. In the peace process it was only after the Oslo Accords that the EU managed to carve out a role for itself as a 'paymaster' and political sponsor of the Palestinians and their organizations. As previously underlined, the assistance from the EU to the Palestinians became a crucial support for the Palestinians, especially during the period when the peace process was stalling. The EU remained constant and secured the livelihood of the Palestinians and helped them to resist external pressure. Between 1993 and 2001, the EU remained committed to the Palestinians, but politically it has still been operating within the frameworks designed by others, in this case the USA and Israel.

Also in relation to the peace process, the appointment of a special envoy was perhaps an act more directed at the EU's domestic audience than with any serious hopes of gaining more influence in the process. Admittedly, it was an improvement on the 'troika travels', but the level of influence the office of the envoy can yield must remain questionable. Having said this, Mr Moratinos is known and trusted by the parties in the Middle East, and he is able to convey messages from the EU—if indeed there are any. Still, it is symbolic, or perhaps symptomatic, that 'Moratinos always turns up when Dennis Ross has left', as one Arab diplomat said, referring to the US envoy. The office of the High Representative and/or the Commission for External Relations are the key actors when it comes to representing the EU and EU's interests. If the EU was intent on bringing its mark to bear on the peace process, and contributing to shaping events, it would be these actors who would be present on the scene.

The message from high ranking Middle East diplomats (both Arab and Israeli)[1] was that they saw a role for the EU after a comprehensive peace agreement has settled the conflict between Arabs and Israelis. After the peace, the EU may serve a valuable function as a facilitator when it comes to improving, supporting socio-economic development and supporting the interstate relations, perhaps—on a long-term basis —with the EU itself as model. Still, the breakdown of the 'Camp David II' and the new intifada beginning in autumn 2000, make 'after the peace' a long prospect. The EU has so far failed to make a significant difference in relation to the intifada. Several attempts to bring the two parties closer and broker cease-fire agreements have led to naught, including a solo initiative by Germany in August 2001 (Haberman 2001: A10). Moreover, it can be assumed that the economic activities related to the Barcelona Process will be mostly of a cosmetic nature until a degree of tranquillity falls over the Israel–Palestinian conflict. It is still too early to speculate on what the implications of the attacks on the USA in September 2001 might have for the EU's role in the conflict, but it is symptomatic that the pressure put on Israel in October 2001 came from the USA. The USA wanted Israel to demonstrate an accommodating attitude towards the Palestinians in order to make it possible for the US to keep its coalition together.

EU and the Mediterranean
The first approach to the Mediterranean region during the 1950s and 1960s was conducted in a somewhat sporadic and piecemeal fashion with the EC establishing bilateral relations with countries in the Middle East and in North Africa. The main driving force was the colonial past of European countries, notably France. The non-EC states were clearly disadvantaged in these negotiations as they alone were forced to conduct bilateral negotiations with the EC member states *en bloc*—an approach the EC/EU has maintained over the years. Hardly surprising, the Middle East states were unable to organize themselves into larger blocks.

---

1.   In private conversations with the authors.

The launch of the Global Mediterranean Policy in 1972 was mainly motivated by a continued rise in Community exports to the Middle East since the end of the 1960s. However, with the oil crises of the 1970s, attention soon shifted to the oil-producing states, and the debacle surrounding OPEC. Though relations were maintained with the Mediterranean countries, no noteworthy initiatives were taken by the EC/EPC during the 1980s.

In the aftermath of the Gulf War, the EC inaugurated a 'New Mediterranean Policy' in 1990. As mentioned in Chapter 4, some of the protocols were to be renegotiated within two years, and there was a strong interest by the EC to strengthen its relations with the region further. The goal was to contribute to the stabilization of the area and to the avoidance of any similar conflicts in future. Dramatic changes in international relations forced the EU to focus on other issues, such as Russia, Eastern and Central Europe—and inwards for some time. The 1995 Barcelona Declaration marked a substantial step forward in the EU's relations with the region. Barcelona was a clear signal that the EU would like to 'go it alone' without the US and the new approach differed in its common, multilateral framework for the Mediterranean states and with its three dimensions of politics, economics and culture.

So, what then has been the overall development of the relations with the Mediterranean? The focus appears to be primarily on sustaining trade relations, and supporting a stabilization of the region by various types of assistance, such as financial and technical. It was only in the post-Cold War era that the EU sought—and indeed was able—to unite behind the establishment of not only independent relations, that is without the USA, but also an enhancement of its international profile. Though the EU will always have interests in maintaining at least cordial relations with the Middle East—for one thing because of its geographical proximity—yet priorities do change.

During the Cold War, the Middle East and North Africa were strategic top priorities. Reliable access to energy resources seen in the context of the Soviet build-up made the EU and the US extremely sensitive to instability in the region. It was a question of the survival of the West, should a conflict break out. Today, the security problem connected to the region has changed dramatically. From an EU perspective, the security problem has turned from hard to soft security. At the moment, instability in the region is now primarily caused by socio-political problems in or between the countries of the region. Managing these types of conflicts for the EU implies new challenges, such as the perceived threat of mass migration caused by low living standards and political oppression. In other words, the threat to the EU would thus arise mainly from these conflicts and as such constitute a possible spillover.

To summarize, one could argue that the Barcelona Process—the EU's approach to the area, and its strategy for pursuing its interests—is indeed a constructive initiative, and it has the noble purpose of supporting socio-economic development and assisting the neighbouring region on its path to political liberalization. However, the problems facing the Middle East—and the interests of the EU—are the problems of today, and the strategy of the Barcelona experience is a long-term one. So, as mentioned in Chapter 6, the EU is trying to address present-day problems with long-term planning. In a sense this goes against EU interests and though the Arab world may be very willing to accept the assistance, the political support and improved relations provided by the EU, the focus will inevitably return to the fact that the level of political and economic integration in the Arab world is very low.

The Actorness of the EU in the Middle East

Sjöstedt's work on 'actorness' has been referred to several times in this book. The conclusion is that the EU possesses autonomy, as it appears clearly as an entity in the international environment.[2] The EU is seen as an actor in its own right by all states in the Middle East, and they all have diplomatic relations with the Union. To be regarded as an international actor depends on the 'actor capability', that is, the unit's capacity to behave actively and deliberately in relation to other actors in the international system.

Though the EU clearly possesses these qualities, it still differs from a superpower[3] on several counts. First, coordinating a common foreign policy stand for its fifteen member states remains a complicated exercise, although these problems are gradually being overcome. Secondly, the resources allocated to the EU's foreign policy activities are generally limited, which naturally means that the EU has to prioritize between, for example, the Eastern Enlargement, the Balkans, Africa,

2.   Autonomy implies that the unit is discernible from its environment, and that it has a minimal degree of cohesion.
3.   For a discussion of definitions of states, see Handel 1990: ch. 1.

and the Middle East. It is safe to say that within the EU, issues related to enlargement and Eastern Europe have more popular appeal, and are much higher on the political agenda than are issues related to the Middle East, at least until 11 September 2001.

Chapter 1 concluded that the EU's mere presence has created expectations among the other actors in the international community, which more often than not, have been unmet in the past, and thus have created frustrations. This is especially so with the Arab states. Nevertheless, the Union does 'make a difference' in foreign policy, not least in the foreign policy of the states in the Middle East. During the Cold War the Arab states have looked to the EU as a third option to the USA and the Soviet Union, and today, the EU is often perceived as the only alternative to the US hegemony of the region. Moreover, the new CFSP structure which has been put in place after Maastricht, Amsterdam and Helsinki has given the EU the dynamism and instruments needed in order potentially to speak of a genuine European foreign and security policy at a great power level. With some caution, while one could argue that the EU in time could be turned into a superpower, but this transformation will demand political will from the member states. With the Humboldt speech by German foreign minister Joschka Fischer (12 May 2000) and the following 'visions' by European statesmen a qualitatively new era of the European integration process is signalled. The EU possesses the qualities needed to play a more active and coherent role in the Middle East than it does today, but apparently it has chosen not to do so.

The Future

First, the future for the EU in the Middle East lies in the time after the settlement of the various conflicts between Israel and the Arab world as well as after the trauma of 11 September 2001 has been overcome. Secondly, if the EU wishes to gain serious influence in the region, the prerequisite is for the EU to muster the political will to make a coordinated and long-term effort, and invest sufficient resources in the projects as well.

On the one hand, a political initiative introduced as a long-term commitment, which fails after a limited amount of time due to other priorities and changing whims of the institutions and changing leadership of the EU will no doubt damage the reputation of the EU seriously. On the other hand, the EU is not alone in deciding on and defining its role. First, the Arab world must approve of the initiatives, and one must assume that a special relationship, if it was to emerge, would necessitate an adherence to concepts such as human rights and democratization. Indeed, these may be two of the most serious obstacles to the future of the relationship. Should the EU appear not to be 'constant in its favours', it will be a let down for the Arab world. Still, there will be other actors which may be interested in establishing relations with the Arab world, such as Asia, individual EU member states, and perhaps Russia depending on her financial situation.

Secondly, Israel must see advantages in a long-term partnership with the EU and revise its perception of the EU as a monolith. The EU–Israeli relationship has been troubled by many incidents where the EC/EU has damaged its possibility to appear as an 'honest broker'. Still, there should be a potential for mutual understanding, as Israel has much closer cultural and historical links to Europe than does the Arab world, and Israel's economic links to the EU is second only to its economic links to the US.

The role of the US can be analysed from several perspectives. A somewhat daring analysis is to follow Brzezinski's (1997) interpretation of international relations theory, and argue that as long as the global interests of the US is to keep its (world) hegemony, the interests of the US are neither peace and stability in the Middle Eastern region, nor a larger role for the EU. A comprehensive peace would undermine the arguments for US military presence in the region, and deliver ample opportunity for the EU to challenge the hegemonic status of the US. From this ultra realist perspective, the future of the Middle East looks gloomy since the chances of a peaceful region are thus substantially reduced.

'The Middle East' has been defined here as the Mashreq and the Gulf. The reason why this definition was chosen was, among other things, to emphasize that the link between the Mashreq and the Gulf is stronger on several accounts than with North Africa. One important example is in relation to the peace process, where the political and/or economic influence and assistance of Gulf States great and small are brought to bear on the process. Furthermore, the EU should consider whether future attempts to support political and economic integration in the region might not be better served if the EU accepts the common historical and cultural cohesiveness of the region.

These definitions and arguments can of course be challenged and criticized, but such a debate will lead to a more nuanced understanding of both the EU's way of conducting its external relations and of the Middle East.

Summing up, the prospect for the future role of the EU in the Middle East is constrained by the following factors:

- the overall political framework being governed by US hegemony;
- the relationship with one of the conflicting powers (Israel) being strained;
- the security political importance of the region having been diminished since the end of the Cold War;
- the relatively large cultural divergences between the Arab world and Europe concerning human rights and democracy;
- the EU member states still not being totally in accordance on how to define the EU's interests and level of involvement in the region. It is expected that the EU will concentrate its energy on the Barcelona Process, rather than taking new initiatives in the Middle East.

The Union has delivered a substantial contribution to the peace process by financially securing the Palestinian Authority. Also, the EU's Barcelona initiative is basically a scheme for long-term stability in the region, partially inspired by the EU's own past in bringing two arch enemies (Germany and France) together, first economically, then politically. One can safely assume that the EU will contribute significantly to the reconstruction of Iraq when at last sanctions are lifted. In sum, the EU has already made quite a contribution and is doing so now to peace and stability in the Middle East. It will no doubt continue this work, but the EU is not in a position to enforce peace.

Bibliography

Aliboni, Roberto
    1996   'Migration: A Threat to European Security?', *European Brief*, pp. 30-31.
Aliboni, Roberto, George Joffé and Tim Niblock (eds.)
    1996   *Security Challenges in the Mediterranean Region* (London: Frank Cass).
Allen, David, and Alfred Pijpers (eds.)
    1984   *European Foreign Policy Making and the Arab-Israeli Conflict* (Dordrecht: Martinus Nijhoff).
Allen, David, and Michael Smith
    1984   'Europe, the United States and the Arab–Israeli Conflict', in Allen and Pijpers 1984: 187-211.
    1990   'Western Europe's Presence in the Contemporary International Arena', *Review of International Studies* 16.1: 19-39.
Anonymous
    2000   'GCC Economies: Time for Revival', Middle East, London: 5-8 (http://proquest.umi.com).
Amirahmadi, Hooshang (ed.)
    1993   *Iran and the Arab World* (New York: St Martin's Press).
Archer, Clive
    1994   *Organizing Europe. The Institutions of Integration* (London: Edward Arnold, 2nd edn).
Armstrong, Karen
    1998   *Jerusalem. Tro, historie, politik* (Copenhagen: Munksgaard, Rosinante).
Azzam, Maha
    1991   'The Gulf Crisis: Perceptions in the Muslim World', *International Affairs* 67.3: 473-85.
Baram, Amatzia
    2000   'The Effect of Iraqi Sanctions: Statistical Pitfalls and Responsibility', *The Middle East Journal* 54.2: 194-223.
Baylis, John, and Steve Smith (eds.)
    1997   *The Globalization of World Politics* (London: Oxford University Press).
Bender, Johan
    1974   *Palæstinaproblemet 1955-74* (Copenhagen: Gyldendals Forlag).
Beyerle, Shaazka
    1998–99   'Notebook: The EU and the Peace Process', http://proquest.umi.com *Europe*, Washington, 382: 53-54.

Blank, Stephen
  2000   'The Mediterranean and Its Security Agenda', *Mediterranean Quarterly*
            11.1: 24-48.
Birkelbach
  1972   *Davignion og Werner-rapporterne* (Copenhagen: Forlaget Mikro).
Bonvicini, Gianni
  1983   'Italy: An Integrationist Perspective', in Hill 1983: 71-84.
Brandenburg, Uwe
  1994   'The European Union and the Gulf Cooperation Council: Cooperation or
            Conflict?', *European Access* 2 (April): 10-12.
Bretherton, Charlotte, and John Vogler
  1999   *The European Union as a Global Actor* (London: Routledge).
Brzezinski, Zbigniew
  1997   *The Grand Chessboard* (London: Basic Books).
Burkay, Kemal
  1997   'The Kurdish Question: Its History and Present Situation', in Høiris Ole,
            and Yürükel Sefa Martin (eds.), *Contrasts and Solutions in the Middle
            East* (Aarhus: Aarhus University Press): 462-73.
Calvocoressi, Peter
  1982   *World Politics Since 1945* (London: Longman, 4th edn).
Chalabi, Fadhil J.
  1997–98   'OPEC: An Obituary', *Foreign Policy,* Winter: 126-41.
Cohen, A.
  1996   'Cairo, Dimona and the June 1967 War', *Middle East Journal* 50.2: 190-
            210.
Copenhagen Report, The
  1973   *Bulletin of the EC*, 9-1973: 14-21.
Darwish, Adel
  2000   'Fortress Saddam Revisited', *The Middle East Journal*, London, May: 13-
            14.
Davignon Report, The
  1970   'Report by the Foreign Ministers of the Member States on the Problems
            of Political Unification', *Bulletin of the EC*, 11-1970: 9-14.
De la Serre, Françoise, and Philippe M. Defarges
  1983   'France: A Penchant for Leadership', in Hill 1983: 56-70.
Delors, Jacques
  1991   'European Integration and Security', *Survival* 33.2: 125-39.
Dinan, Desmond
  1999   *Ever Closer Union. An Introduction to European Integration* (London:
            Macmillan, 2nd edn).
Dosenrode, Søren von
  1993   *Westeuropäische Kleinstaaten in der EG und EPZ* (Zürcher Beiträge zur
            Politischen Wissenschaft, Band 18; Chur: Verlag Rüegger).
  2000   *Dansk Udenrigspolitik*, Rådet for Europæisk Politik 1/2000, Systime,
            Aarhus.
Dunbabin, J.P.D.
  1994a   *The Post-Imperial Age: The Great Powers and the Wider World* (London:
            Longman).

1994b   *The Cold War: The Great Powers and their Allies* (London: Longman).

EC Commission
1982   *The European Community and the Arab World* (Luxembourg: Europe
             Information).

Edwards, Geoffrey
1984   'Britain', in Allen and Pijpers 1984: 47-60.

Esposito, John L., and J. Voll
1996   *Islam and Democracy* (Oxford: Oxford University Press).

European Parliament
1999a   POLI + 115EN: 'The Middle East Peace Process and the European
             Union—Working Paper', The European Parliament, Directorate General
             for Research.

European Parliament (1999b), POLI + B 116EN: 'The Price for Non-Peace: The European
             Union in the Middle East', The European Parliament, Directorate General
             for Research.

Eurostat Yearbook
2000   *A Statistical Guide to Europe* (Luxembourg: Office for Official
             Publications of the European Communities).

Fenech, Dominic
1997   'The Relevance of European Security Structures to the Mediterranean
             (and Vice Versa)', in Gillespie (ed.) 1997: 149-77.

Findlay, Allan M.
1994   *The Arab World* (London: Routledge).

George, Alan
1998a   'A Decisive Year for GCC-EU Relations?' *The Middle East Journal,*
             London, March: 32-33.
1998b   'Human Rights Sidelined in the Euro-Med Agreements', *The Middle East
             Journal*, London, November: 12.

George, Stephen
1996   *Politics and Policy in the European Union* (Oxford: Oxford University
             Press, 3rd edn).

Gillespie, Richard (ed.)
1997   *The Euro-Mediterranean Partnership: Political and Economic
             Perspectives* (London: Frank Cass).

Greilsammer, Ilan, and Joseph Weiler
1984   'European Political Cooperation and the Palestinian-Israeli Conflict: An
             Israeli Perspective', in Allen and Pijpers 1984: 121-61.

Gomez, Richardo
1998   'The EU's Mediterranean Policy: Common Foreign Policy by the Back
             Door?, in John Peterson and Helene Sjursen (eds.), *A Common Foreign
             Policy for Europe? Competing Visions of the CFSP* (London: Routledge):
             133-52.

Groom, A.J.R., and Margot Light (eds.)
1994   *Contemporary International Relations: A Guide to Theory* (London:
             Pinter Publishers).

Guttman, Robert J.
1998–99   'Europe Interview: European Union Special Envoy Miguel Moratinos',
             Europe, Washington, December/January: 30-31.

Haberman, Clyde
    2001   'New Middle East Peace Bid Brokered by German Envoy', *New York Times*, 22 August: 10A.
Halliday, Fred
    1991   'The Gulf War and its Aftermath: First Reflections, *International Affairs* 67.2: 223-35.
    1998   'Western Europe and the Iranian Revolution, 1979-97: An Elusive Normalization', in Robertson (ed.) 1998: 130-51.
Handel, Michael
    1990   *Weak States in the International System* (London: Frank Cass).
Hermann, Richard K.
    1994   'Russian Policy in the Middle East: Strategic Change and Tactical Contradictions', *Middle East Journal* 48.3, Summer: 455-74.
Hill, Christopher
    1993   'The Capability-Expectations Gap, or Conceptualising Europe's International Role', *Journal of Common Market Studies* 31.3: 305-27.
Hill, Christopher (ed.)
    1983   *National Foreign Politicies and European Political Cooperation* (London: George, Allen & Unwin).
    1996   *The Actors in Europe's Foreign Policy* (London: Routledge).
Hollis, Rosemary
    1997   'Europe and the Middle East: Power by Stealth?', *International Affairs* 73.1: 15-29.
Hourani, Albert
    1994   *Det Arabiske Folks Historie* (Copenhagen: Gyldendalske Boghandel, Nordiske Forlag A-S).
Hubel, Helmut
    1991   'Die Rolle der Supermächte: Der Nahe und Mittlere Osten im Ost-West-Konflikt', in Gert Krell and Bernd W. Kubbig (eds.), *Krieg & Frieden am Golf* (Frankfurt am Main: Fischer Taschenbuch Verlag).
Hudson, Michael M.
    1992   'The Middle East under Pax Americana: How New, How Orderly?', *Third World Quarterly* 13.2: 301-16.
    1996   'To Play the Hegemon: Fifty Years of US Policy towards the Middle East', *Middle East Journal* 50.3: 329-44.
Ifestos, Panayotis
    1987   *European Political Cooperation: Towards a Framework of Supranational Diplomacy?* (Aldershot: Avebury).
Imperiali, Claude, and Pierre Agate
    1984   'France', in Allen and Pijpers 1984: 1-18.
Ismael, Tareq
    1986   *International Relations of the Contemporary Middle East: A Study in World Politics* (Syracuse, NY: Syracuse University Press).
Jabarwi, Ali
    1995   'The Triangle of Conflict', *Foreign Policy* 100, Fall: 92-100.
Jawad, Haiifaa A.
    1992   *Euro-Arab Relations: A Study in Collective Dimplomacy* (Reading: Ithaca Press).

Jensen, Michael Irving, and Andreas Laursen
2000   *Arafats Palæstina* (Odense: Odense Universitets Forlag).
Joffé, G.
1997   'Southern Attitudes towards an Integrated Mediterranean Region', in
           Gillespie (ed.) 1997: 12-33.
Karawan, Ibrahim A.
1994   'Arab Dilemmas in the 1990s,: Breaking Taboos and Searching for Sign-
           posts', *Middle East Journal* 48.3, Summer: 433-54.
1997   'The Islamist Impasse', *Adelphi Paper 314*, The Institute for Strategic
           Studies.
Keating, Patrick
1984   'Ireland', in Allen and Pijpers 1984: 18-31.
Kegley, Charles W., and Eugene R. Wittkopf
1995   *World Politic: Trends and Traditions* (New York: St Martins Press, 5th
           edn).
Keohane, Robert O. (ed.)
1986   *Neorealism and its Critics* (New York: Columbia University Press).
Khader, Bichara
1984   'Europe and the Arab-Israeli Conflict: An Arab Perspective', in Allen and
           Pijpers 1984: 161-87.
Krämer, G.
1995   'Islam and Pluralism', in B. Korany, R. Brynen and P. Noble (eds.),
           Political Liberalisation and Democratisation in the Arab World:
           Theoretical Perspectives (Boulder, CO: Lynne Rienner Publishers): I,
           113-23, bibliography ch. 6, part 2.
Krasner, Stephen
1997   'The Middle East and the End of the Cold War', in Laura Guazzone (ed.),
           The Middle East in Global Change (London: Macmillan).
Laqueur, Walter, and Barry Rubin (eds.)
1995   *The Israel-Arab Reader: A Documentary History of the Middle East*
           Conflict (New York: Penguin Group, 5th edn): The Balfour Declaration,
           p. 16.
Laursen, Finn, and Sophie Hoonacker (eds.)
1992   *The Intergovernmental Conference on Political Union* (Maastricht:
           European Institute of Public Administration).
Lesser, Ian O.
1999   'The Changing Mediterranean Security Environment: A Transatlantic
           Perspective', in G. Joffé (ed.), *Perspectives on Development: The Euro-*
           Mediterranean Partnership (London: Frank Cass): 212-29.
Lister, Marjory
1988   *The European Community and the Developing World* (Aldershot:
           Avebury).
London Report, The
1981   *Bulletin of the EC*, S.3/81: 14-17.
Lukacs, Yehuda (ed.)
1992   *The Israeli-Palestinian Conflict: A Documentary Record 1967–1990*
           (Cambridge: Cambridge University Press).

Luxembourg Report, The
    1970   'Report by the Foreign Ministers of the Member States on the Problems of Political Unification', *Bulletin of the EC* 11-1970: 9-14.
Macleod, I., I.D. Hendry and Stephen Heyett
    1996   *The External Relations of the European Communities: A Manual of Law and Practice* (Oxford: Clarendon Press).
Maksoud, Clovis
    1995   'Peace Process or Puppet Show?', *Foreign Policy* 100, Fall: 117-25.
Mansfield, Peter
    1991   *A History of the Middle East* (London: Penguin Books).
    1992   *The Arabs* (London: Penguin Books, 3rd edn).
Maoz, Moshe, and Avner Yaniv (eds.)
    1986   *Syria under Assad: Domestic Constraints and Regional Risks* (London: Croom Helm).
Martin-Diaz, Alicia
    1999   'Middle East Peace Process and the European Union', Working paper, European Parliament, Luxembourg.
Massalha, Omar
    1994   *Towards the Long-Promised Peace* (London: Saqi Books).
Menashri, David (ed.)
    1998   *Central Asia Meets the Middle East* (London: Frank Cass).
Milton-Edwards, Beverley
    2000   *Contemporary Politics in the Middle East* (Cambridge: Polity Press).
Mitchell Report
            http://www.jmcc.org./new/01/Apr/mitchel.htm
Monnet, Jean
    1987   *Mit Liv* (Copenhagen: Forum).
Niblock, Tim
    1998   'Democratization: A Theoretical and Practical Debate', *British Journal of Middle Eastern Studies*, Exeter, November: 221-33 (http://proquest.umi).
Nirumand, Bahman (ed.)
    1991   *Sturm im Golf* (Reinbek bei Hamburg: Rowohlt Verlag).
Nørretranders, Bjarne
    1984   'Dobbeltbeslutningen', Det Udenrigspolitiske Selskab, *Udenrigspolitiske Skrifter*, 16.3 (Copenhagen: Schulz).
Nugent, Neil
    1994   *The Government and Politics of the European Union* (Houndmills: Macmillan, 4th edn).
Nuttall, Simon J.
    2000   *European Foreign Policy* (Oxford: Oxford University Press).
Owen, Roger
    1992   *State, Power and Politics in the Making of the Modern Middle East* (London: Routledge).
Patten, Christopher
    2000   'The EU's Evolving Foreign Policy Dimension: The CESDP after Helsinki', speech delivered at the Joint Meeting of the European Parliament Foreign Affairs Committee with Members of the NATO Parliamentary Assembly, 22 February.

Parfitt, Trevor
    1997   'Europe's Mediterranean Designs: An Analysis of the Euromed Relationship with Special Reference to Egypt', *Third World Quarterly* 18.5: 865-81.

Peters, Joel
    1999   'Europe and the Middle East Peace Process: Emerging from the Sidelines', in Stavridis *et al.* 1999.

Polk, William R.
    1991   *The Arab World Today* (Cambridge, MA: Harvard University Press).

Preston, C.
    1997   *Enlargement and Integration in the European Union* (London: Routledge).

Raeymaker, Omer de
    1984   'Belgium', in Allen and Pijpers 1984: 60-80.

Regelsberger, Elfriede, Philippe de Schoutheete de Tervarent and Wolfgang Wessels (eds.)
    1997   *Foreign Policy of the European Union: From ECP to CFSP and Beyond* (London: Lynne Rienner).

Report from the Danish UN ambassador to the Danish Foreign Ministry no. 610.K.54, 1969.

Roberson, B.A. (ed.)
    1998   *The Middle East and Europe: The Power Deficit* (London: Routledge).

Rummel, R., and W. Wessels
    1983   'Federal Republic of Germany: New Responsibilities, Old Constraints', in Hill (ed.) 1983: 34-55.

Safran, Nadav
    1992   'Dimensions of the Middle East Problem: Before and After the Gulf War', in Roy Macridis (ed.), *Foreign Policy in World Politics* (Englewood Cliffs, NJ: Prentice Hall): 357-405.

Saleh, Nivien
    1999   'The European Union and the Gulf States: A Growing Partnership', http://www.proquest.umi.com. Also published in *Middle East Policy*; Washington, October: 50-71.

Salibi, Kamal
    1998   *The History of Modern Jordan* (New York: I.B. Tauris).

Sayigh, Yezid
    1991   'The Gulf Crisis: Why the Arab Regional Order Failed', *International Affairs* 67.3: 487-507.

Scott, Lenn
    1997   'International History 1945–90', in Baylis and Smith (eds.) 1997: 71-89.

Segal, Aaron
    1991   'Spain and the Middle East: A 15-Year Assessment', *The Middle East Journal* 45.2, Spring: 250-64.

Selim, Mohammad E.
    1997   'Egypt and the Euro-Mediterranean Partnership: Strategic Choice or Adaptive Mechanism', in Gillespie (ed.) 1997: 64-93.

Serfaty, Simon
    1998   'Bridging the Gap across the Atlantic: Europe and the United States in the Persian Gulf', http://www.proquest.umi.com. Also published in *The Middle East Journal*, Washington, Summer: 337-50.

Sharm el-Sheikh Fact-Finding Commission, *see* Mitchell Report.

Shirley, Edward G.
1994   'The Iran Policy Trap', *Foreign Policy*, http://www.proquest.umi.com, Washington, Fall: 1-9.
Shlaim, A.
1997   'The Protocol of Sèvres, 1956: Autonomy of a War Plot', *International Affairs* 73.3: 509-30.
Silvestri, Stefano
1984   'Italy', in Allen and Pijpers 1984: 31-37.
Sjöstedt, Gunnar
1977   *The External Role of the European Community* (Farnborough: Gower).
Skovgaard-Petersen, Jakob
1995   *Moderne Islam: Muslimer i Cairo* (Copenhagen: Gyldendalske Boghandel, Nordiske Forlag A/S).
Smith, Charles D.
1992   *Palestine and the Arab-Israeli Conflict* (New York: St Martin's Press, 2nd edn).
Soedentorp, Ben
1984   'The Netherlands', in Allen and Pijpers 1984: 37-47.
Solana, Javier
2000   'The Development of a Common Foreign and Security Policy and the Role of the High Representative', speech delivered at the Danish Institute of International Affairs (DUPI), Christiansborg Palace, Copenhagen 11 February.
SOU
1996   Eet år med EU—Svenska statstjänstemäns erfarenheter av arbetet i EU, Statens offentliga utredningar, 1996: 6, Utrikesdepartementet, Stockholm.
Spencer, Claire
1999   'Security Implications of the EMPI', in G. Joffé (ed.), *Perspectives on Development: The Euro-Mediterranean Partnership* (London: Frank Cass): 202-12.
Stavridis, Stelios, Theodore Couloumbis, Thanos Veremis and Neville Waites (eds.)
1999   *The Foreign Policies of the European Union's Mediterranean States and Applicant Countries in the 1990s* (Houndmills: Macmillan Press).
Steinbach, Udo
1984   'Germany', in Allen and Pijpers 1984: 91-107.
The Economist
1995   'A New Crusade', 2 December.
The Economist Intelligence Unit
1996–97   *Country Profile: Jordan.*
Thune, Christian
1984   'Denmark', in Allen and Pijpers 1984: 80-91.
Tindemans, Leo
1976   Den europæiske Union: rapport fra hr. Leo Tindemans til Det europæiske Råd, Luxembourg, København, Udenrigsministeriet, Ministeriet for Udenrigshandel og Udviklingssamarbejde.
Tovias, Alfred
1996   'Why the North Must Start Taking the South More Seriously', *European Brief,* March: 30-31.

Venice Declaration
1980   *Bulletin of the EC*, 6-1980: 10-11, point 1.1.6.
Voorhoeve, Joris
1985   *Peace, Profits and Principles* (Dordrecht: Martinus Nijhoff).
Waites, Neville, and Stelios Stavridis
1999   'The European Union and Mediterranean Member States', in Stavridis *et al.* (eds.) 1999: 22-39.
Waltz, Kenneth N.
1979   *Theory of International Politics* (New York: McGraw-Hill).
Weiss, B.G., and A.H. Green
1988   *A Survey of Arab History* (Cairo: The American University in Cairo Press, rev. edn).
Wheeler, Nicholas P.
1997   'Humanitarian Intervention and World Politics', in Baylis and Smith (eds.) 1997: 391-409.
White, Gregory
1999   'Encouraging Immigration: A Political Economy of Europe's Efforts to Discourage North African Immigration', *Third World Quarterly*, London, August: 839-54 (1-12).
Yapp, M.E.
1994   *The Making of the Modern Near East 1792–1923* (London: Longman).
1996   *The Near East Since the First World War* (London: Longman, 2nd edn).
Young, Penny
1998   'Syria Signs with Europe', *Middle East* 283, London, October: 30-31.

Websites

Bulletin of the European Union (formerly the European Community)
    http://europa.eu.int/abc/doc/off/bull/en/welcom.int
European Institutions in general
    http://europa.eu.int/
    http://europa.eu.int/eu-lex/en/treaties/index.html.
Europe on the Move
    http://europa.eu.int/comm/dg10/publications/brochures/move/index_en.html.
General Report on the Activities of the European Union (former European Community)
    http://europa.eu.int/abc/off/rg/en/welcom.html, various years.
Treaty Establishing the European Community
    http://europa.eu.int/eu-lex/en/treaties/index.html, or *Official Journal* C 340, 10 November 1997: 145-72.
Treaty on European Union
    http://europa.eu.int/eu-lex/en/treaties/index.html, or *Official Journal* C 340, 10 November 1997: 175-308.
Treaty of Nice
    http://europa.eu.int/eu-lex/en/treaties/index.html, or *Official Journal* C 80, 10 March 2001.

General Index

Index of Authors

UNIVERSITY ASSOCIATION FOR CONTEMPORARY EUROPEAN STUDIES
UACES Secretariat, King's College London, Strand, London WC2R 2LS, UK
Tel: +44 (0)20 7240 0206   Fax: +44 (0)20 7836 2350   Email: admin@uaces.org
www.uaces.org

UACES

University Association for Contemporary European Studies

The Association
- Brings together academics involved in researching Europe with representatives of government, industry and the media who are active in European affairs
- Primary organisation for British academics researching the European Union
- Over 600 individual and corporate members from Dept such as Politics, Law, Economics & European Studies, plus over 150 Graduate Students who join as Associate Members

Membership Benefits
- Individual Members eligible for special highly reduced fee for The Journal of Common Market Studies (JCMS)
- Regular Newsletter - events and developments of relevance to members
- Conferences - variety of themes, modestly priced, further reductions for members
- Publications, including the new series *Contemporary European Studies*, launched in 1998
- Research Network, and research conference
- Through the European Community Studies Association (ECSA), access to a larger world wide network
- Information Documentation & Resources eg: The Register of Courses in European Studies and the Register of Research into European Integration

Current Cost of Membership per annum
☛ Individual Members: £25.00   ☛ Associate (Student): £10.00   ☛ Corporate Members: £50.00

APPLICATION FOR MEMBERSHIP OF UACES
Please complete the appropriate details and return the entire form to the address above.

Last Name: _____ First Name: _____ Title (eg Mr): ___

Institution: _____

Faculty / Dept: _____

Institution Address: _____

_____

Work Tel No: _____ Work Fax No: _____

Home Tel No: _____ Home Fax No: _____

E-mail: _____

Address for correspondence if different: _____

_____

Where did you hear about UACES? _____

Signature and Date: _____

PTO TO COMPLETE PAYMENT DETAILS

CES Ad1.doc

UNIVERSITY ASSOCIATION FOR CONTEMPORARY EUROPEAN STUDIES
UACES Secretariat, King's College London, Strand, London WC2R 2LS, UK
Tel: +44 (0)20 7240 0206   Fax: +44 (0)20 7836 2350   Email: admin@uaces.org
www.uaces.org

PAYMENT DETAILS

☛ TO PAY BY CHEQUE*

I wish to pay my membership subscription by cheque. Please make cheques payable to UACES, not King's College.

Please find enclosed a cheque (in pounds sterling) for:
❏ £25 (Individual)   ❏ £10 (Associate - Student)   ❏ £50 (Corporate)

* Please Note: we are no longer able to accept Eurocheques

☛ TO PAY BY CREDIT/DEBIT CARD

I wish to pay my membership subscription by (mark appropriate box):
❏ Visa   ❏ Mastercard   ❏ Eurocard   ❏ Switch   ❏ Solo

I authorise you to debit my Account with the amount of (mark appropriate box):
❏ £25 (Individual)   ❏ £10 (Associate - Student)   ❏ £50 (Corporate)

Signature of cardholder: _____   Date: _____

My Card Number is: ☐☐☐☐ ☐☐☐☐ ☐☐☐☐ ☐☐☐☐ ☐☐☐

Cardholder's Name and Initials*:_____   Cardholder's Title* (eg Mr): _____
*As shown on the card

Expiry Date: ☐☐☐☐   Start Date (if present*): ☐☐☐☐   Issue No. (if present*): ☐
*Usually for Switch and Solo cards

Cardholder's address and postcode (if different from overleaf):
_____

☛ TO PAY BY STANDING ORDER* (UK Bank only)
*This option not available for Corporate or Associate (Student) members

Please complete the details below and return to UACES. We will process the membership application and then forward this authority to your bank. This authority is not a Direct Debit authority (ie we cannot take money out of your bank account without your permission).

To (insert your Bank Name) _____   at (insert your bank address)

_____   (insert Post Code) _____, UK.

Please pay to Lloyds Bank, Pall Mall Branch, 8-10 Waterloo Place, London SW1Y 4BE, UK, in favour of UACES, Account No. 3781242, Sort-Code 30-00-08, on the (insert date, eg 1st) _____ day of (insert month, eg June) _____ , the sum of £25 (TWENTY FIVE POUNDS) and the same sum on the same date each year until countermanded.

Signature: _____   Date: _____

Name: _____

Address: _____

Account No.: _____   Sort-code: _____